Landmarks of world literature

James Joyce

ULYSSES

Landmarks of world literature

General editor: J. P. Stern

JAMES JOYCE

Ulysses

VINCENT SHERRY

Villanova University

CAMBRIDGE
UNIVERSITY PRESS

Published by the Press Syndicate of the University of Cambridge
The Pitt Building, Trumpington Street, Cambridge CB2 1RP
40 West 20th Street, New York NY 10011−4211, USA
10 Stamford Road, Oakleigh, Melbourne 3166, Australia

First published 1994

Printed in Great Britain at the University Press, Cambridge

A catalogue record for this book is available from the British Library

Library of Congress cataloguing in publication data
Sherry, Vincent B.
James Joyce, Ulysses / Vincent Sherry.
        p.   cm. − (Landmarks of world literature)
Includes bibliographical references
ISBN 0 521 42075 X hardback / ISBN 0 521 42136 5 paperback
1. Joyce, James, 1882−1941.   Ulysses.   I. Title.   II. Series.
PR6019.09U697   1995
823'.912 − dc20   93−47122 CIP

ISBN 0 521 42075 X hardback
ISBN 0 521 42136 5 paperback

WG

For Sophia
Consonantia

Contents

Preface

When T. S. Eliot titled his early anthology *"Introducing* James Joyce," he started an ongoing process: *Ulysses* has been reintroduced now to four or five generations. One measure of "landmark" status for a literary work, after all, is its continued capacity to be rediscovered, and *Ulysses* meets that test again and again. Its dimensions seem indeed to have grown with the history of literary criticism in the current century, to each of whose major phases it has responded remarkably well. To the neoclassical standards of high modernism, which continued in the formal intelligence of the New Criticism in the 1950s, it offered its Homeric structure and elaborate schematic imagination; to the post-structuralists of the 1960s and 1970s, it presented a language animated by experimental and convention-dismaying energies; to the new historical critics of the 1980s, it has revealed founding contexts in political and cultural history, here the shifting backgrounds of turn-of-the-century Ireland and the Europe of the Great War of 1914–1918. Reading Joyce's book can be like reliving the literary and intellectual history of the twentieth century, the course of which it has helped to direct perhaps no less effectively than any other single work.

If the proponents of these several methodologies have engaged sometimes in the gang-warfare of successive literary generations, I am less troubled by their oppositional premises. Formalism describes an energy in *Ulysses* no less potent than its deconstructive temper (each side of this counterrhythm lifts and reinforces the other), and attention to the verbal textures of a work need not preclude interest in the shaping occasions of historical place and time. The historical, formalist, and linguistic dimensions of *Ulysses* are the major emphases, in turn, of the three chapters that follow here, which seek, by the end, to blend and balance these several lines of inquiry in a single critical vision. *Ulysses* is one book, even if its centers of energy are various, indeed conflicting.

One of the assumptions in these chapters is that influence can be exerted in radiating rather than pointed or direct ways, and so my acknowledgments to the legacy of Joyce scholarship must be incomplete. The list of critical titles included here under "Further reading" is designed to represent a tradition as well as to cite specific, local debts. Of these the most urgent are owed to the Joyceans who read and commented on this book in manuscript: to A. Walton Litz, Vicki Mahaffey, Robert Spoo, and Michael Groden. Students have also enriched my reading of *Ulysses*: I thank Daniel Hipp, Christopher Segrave-Daly, and, especially, Mara Jeanne Browne. Material support and encouragement have come unstintingly from Villanova University, where I wish to thank Rev. Lawrence Gallen and Rev. Kail Ellis above all. I am grateful to Jennifer Azara for proofreading so well *in extremis*. To J.P. Stern, founding editor of the Landmarks series at Cambridge University Press, I express my gratitude (now, sadly, posthumously) for his invitation and his responses to an early prospectus; to Kevin Taylor, Senior Editor, for critical understanding as well as practical help; and to Katharina Brett, for expediting all business with such care and intelligence. I am reminded by my wife, Hiroko, that life, like *Ulysses*, can be a book of hours; she redeems the time. My daughter, Sophia, responded once to a lengthy disquisition on Joyce's use of ancient legend, on the mythic method in general: "It's like an old shoe – the more you rub it, the deeper it shines." She continues to improve me; I dedicate this book to her, wise also in harmonies.

" 'Wandering Rocks' and the art of gratuity" appeared in a slightly altered version in *James Joyce Quarterly*; I am grateful to the editor for permission to reprint.

Abbreviations

CW	*The Critical Writings of James Joyce*, Ellsworth Mason and Richard Ellmann, eds. 1959. Rpt. Ithaca: Cornell University Press, 1989
D	*"Dubliners": Text, Criticism, and Notes*, Robert Scholes and A. Walton Litz, eds. New York: Viking, 1969.
FW	*Finnegans Wake*. New York: Viking, 1939 (identical pagination with English edition from Faber and Faber, 1939).
Letters I, II, III	*Letters of James Joyce*. Vol. I, Stuart Gilbert, ed. New York: Viking, 1957; reissued with corrections 1966. Vols. II and III, Richard Ellmann, ed. New York: Viking, 1966.
P	*"A Portrait of the Artist as a Young Man": Text, Criticism, and Notes*, Chester G. Anderson, ed. New York: Viking, 1968.
SH	*Stephen Hero*, John J. Slocum and Herbert Cahoon, eds. New York: New Directions, 1944, 1963.

References are by page number to volumes above.
References are by episode and line number to *Ulysses*, Hans Walter Gabler *et al.*, eds. New York and London: Garland Publishing, 1984, 1986. In paperback by Garland, Random House, Bodley Head, and Penguin. (See "Further reading.")

Chronology

	Life and work	Political and cultural history
		Virginia Stephen (Woolf) and Wyndham Lewis born
1882	2 February: James Joyce born in Rathgar, a suburb of Dublin, eldest son to John Stanislaus Joyce, rate collector, and Mary Jane (Murray) Joyce	
1885		Ezra Pound and D. H. Lawrence born; Marx, *Das Kapital*
1886		First Home Rule Bill for Ireland; Irish Party wins 86 of 103 contested seats in Parliament; letters published in London *Times* implicate Charles Stewart Parnell in murder of Lord Frederick Cavendish, but are shown to be forgeries
1887		Nietzsche, *The Genealogy of Morals*
1888	Enrolled at Clongowes Wood College, a Jesuit boarding school, twenty miles west of Dublin	T. S. Eliot born
1890		Ibsen's *Hedda Gabler*; exposure of Parnell's affair with Kitty O'Shea forces Gladstone to withdraw political support; Parnell repudiated by Irish Catholic clergy
1891	Withdrawn from Clongowes in June after father loses his position; writes a verse broadside on the occasion of the death of Charles Stewart Parnell, *Et Tu, Healy!* (none of the copies printed by John Joyce survives)	Death of Parnell
1892	Joyce family moves to Blackrock, halfway between Bray and Dublin	

1893	Enrolled (after brief attendance at the Christian Brothers' school in North Richmond) in Belvedere College, a Jesuit day school, where he compiles brilliant academic record; the Joyces move into Dublin, their fortunes declining	
1894	At Belvedere, wins the first of several exhibition prizes for scholarship	
1895		Trials of Oscar Wilde
1898		Dreyfus Affair in France
1899	Refuses to join a protest of University College students against Yeats's play *The Countess Cathleen*	
1900	Reads "Drama and Life" before the Literary and Historical Society of University College; publishes essay on "Ibsen's New Drama" in the *Fortnightly Review*	Bergson, *Rire (Laughter)*; Freud, *The Interpretation of Dreams*
1901	Attacks the insularity of the Irish Literary Theatre in "The Day of the Rabblement," an essay published in a student pamphlet	Boer War in South Africa; Queen Victoria dies, succeeded by Edward VII; anarchism and strikes in Italy and France; Freud, *The Psychopathology of Everyday Life*; Irish literary renaissance under Yeats, Lady Gregory, George Moore, and AE (George Russell)
1902	Graduates from University College with a degree in modern languages (proficiency in Latin, Italian, French, German, and literary Norwegian); leaves Dublin for Paris (ostensibly to study medicine) in late November	
1903	Compiles his manuscript collection of "Epiphanies" – mainly plotless evocations of mood and place – in Paris between early January and April; returns to Dublin in April, as his mother's last illness begins; publishes twenty-three book reviews for the Dublin *Daily Express* between 11 December 1902 and 19 November 1903; Mary Joyce dies on 13 August	Synge's *In the Shadow of the Glen*, staged at Irish National Theatre, stirs controversy over national art; Henry James, *The Ambassadors*

1904	Begins to revise and expand "A Portrait of the Artist," an essay first written on 7 January and rejected for publication in *Dana*, as *Stephen Hero*; publishes poems in the *Speaker*, *Saturday Review*, *Dana*, *Venture*, and stories in the *Irish Homestead*; teaches in Dalkey at the Clifton School; on 10 June meets Nora Barnacle; on 9 September moves into the Martello Tower with Oliver St. John Gogarty (model for Buck Mulligan) and leaves on 19 September; leaves Dublin with Nora in October, traveling to Paris, Zurich, Trieste, finally to Pola (later in Yugoslavia), and teaches there in Berlitz school	General Strike by anarcho-syndicalists in Italy; Abbey Theatre, Dublin, founded
1905	Transferred to Berlitz school in Trieste; son Giorgio born on 27 July; submits first manuscript of *Dubliners* ("Two Gallants," "A Little Cloud," and "The Dead" still to be written) to Grant Richards and initiates nine-year struggle for publication	
1906	Moves to Rome and works as foreign correspondent in bank; conceives (but cannot write) a short story, "Ulysses," featuring a Dublin Jew named Hunter	
1907	Returns to Trieste and gives private lessons in English; *Chamber Music* (poems) published by Elkin Matthews, London; daughter Lucia Anna born on 26 July; finishes "The Dead" in September and begins to revise *Stephen Hero* as *A Portrait of the Artist as a Young Man*	Women organize to gain suffrage in Europe and America; riots in Dublin after staging of Synge's *Playboy of the Western World*; Picasso's *Demoiselles d'Avignon* and emergence of Cubism in Paris
1909	Returns to Ireland twice, first to arrange a contract with Maunsel & Co. for *Dubliners*, then to manage the Cinematograph Volta, which opened, with the backing of Triestine businessmen, on 20 December	Gertrude Stein, *Three Lives*; Wyndham Lewis, first stories published in Ford Madox (Hueffer) Ford's *English Review*

1910	Returns to Trieste in January; publication of *Dubliners* postponed due to fears of Maunsel & Co.	Suffragette riots in London; Forster, *Howards End*
1911		"Imagism" promulgated in London by Pound, T. E. Hulme, H. D., and others; Futurist Exhibition in London
1912	Returns (with his family) in July for last time to Ireland, visiting Galway and Dublin; *Dubliners* destroyed by printer, prompting Joyce's broadside on Irish cultural parochialism, "Gas From a Burner"	
1913	Begins correspondence with Ezra Pound, who interests Dora Marsden, editor of the *New Freewoman* (later the *Egoist*), in manuscript chapters of *Portrait*	Meeting at Rotunda Rink in Dublin of Irish National Volunteers, active in later Easter Rising; Lawrence, *Sons and Lovers*; Einstein's Theory of Relativity; first issues of Dora Marsden's *New Freewoman* (later, the *Egoist*)
1914	*Portrait* serialized in the *Egoist* from 2 February to 1 September 1915; begins work on *Ulysses* in March, but puts it aside to write his Ibsenesque play *Exiles*; *Dubliners* published by Grant Richards on 15 June	Irish Home Rule Bill revived but blocked; *Blast* (Lewis's magazine of English Vorticism) publishes first of two issues in London; Austrian Archduke Ferdinand and wife assassinated in Sarajevo; World War begins in August
1915	Moves with his family in June to Zurich, pledging neutrality to the Swiss authorities; finishes *Exiles*; receives money from British Royal Literary Fund through recommendations of Pound, Yeats, and Edmund Gosse	Zeppelin attacks on London; Italy joins Allies; Lawrence, *The Rainbow* (suppressed); Ford, *The Good Soldier*; *Blast 2* (July, War Number)
1916	Receives grant from British Treasury Fund; *Portrait* published in New York by B. W. Huebsch	Lewis's *Tarr* serialized in the *Egoist*; emergence of "dada" in Zurich; Easter Rising in Dublin
1917	*Portrait* published in London by Egoist Press; eight poems published in *Poetry* (Chicago); receives first (anonymous) gift from Harriet Shaw Weaver, eventually his major patron; receives money in March for the manuscript of *Exiles* from John Quinn, a New York lawyer, who writes favorable review of *Portrait* in *Vanity Fair* in May; worsening of eye troubles followed by eye operation late in the summer and three-month recuperation in Locarno	October Revolution in Russia; United States enters World War; Eliot, *Prufrock and Other Observations*

1918	Returns to Zurich and receives monthly stipend from Mrs. Harold McCormick; organizes (with Claud Sykes) the English Players, produces Oscar Wilde's *Importance of Being Earnest*, but argues with leading actor and enters into lawsuits; first episodes of *Ulysses* serialized in the *Little Review* (New York), completing more than half the book by December 1920; *Exiles* published by Grant Richards in London and Huebsch in New York	General Strike and influenza epidemic in Switzerland; Armistice on 11 November; Spengler, *The Decline of the West* (vol. 1)
1919	Five installments of *Ulysses* published in the *Egoist*; subsidy withdrawn by Mrs. McCormick; returns with family to Trieste in October, teaching English at commercial school and working intensively on *Ulysses*	Treaty of Versailles; National Socialist Party founded in Germany; Fascisti formed in Italy by Mussolini; Red and White armies battle in Russia; Shakespeare & Co. founded in Paris by Sylvia Beach
1920	Meets Pound in Sirmione; moves with family to Paris; serial publication of *Ulysses* in the *Little Review* discontinued (at episode 13, "Nausicaa") on charge of pornography by the Society for the Prevention of Vice in New York	League of Nations established; separate parliaments proposed for North and South by the Government of Ireland Act (rejected by the South); Pound, *Hugh Selwyn Mauberley*; Eliot, *The Sacred Wood*; Lewis meets and draws Joyce in Paris
1921	Withdraws manuscript of *Ulysses* from consideration for publication by Huebsch, in New York, following the *Little Review* scandal; part of typescript of episode 15 ("Circe") burned by typist's husband; forms plan to have *Ulysses* published in Paris by Sylvia Beach's Shakespeare & Co.	War reparations imposed on Germany; Fascists elected to Italian Parliament; Treaty between England and Ireland; Pirandello, *Six Characters in Search of an Author*
1922	*Ulysses* published in Paris on 2 February, Joyce's fortieth birthday; Valery Larbaud's essay on *Ulysses*, keyed to Joyce's (still secret) schema, published in *Nouvelle Revue Française*	Irish Free State proclaimed; Fascists' "march on Rome" and Mussolini's appointment as Prime Minister; Spengler, *The Decline of the West* (vol. 2); Woolf, *Jacob's Room*; Eliot, *The Waste Land*

1923	Begins to write *Finnegans Wake*; visits England in summer	
1924	Severe eye trouble, continuing for the rest of Joyce's life; first fragment of *Finnegans Wake* (then *work in progress*) in the *Transatlantic Review* (Paris)	Lenin dies; Stalin comes to power; Hitler, imprisoned for nine months, writes *Mein Kampf*
1925	Second fragment from *Finnegans Wake* published in the *Criterion* (London); first version of "Anna Livia Plurabelle" section from *Finnegans Wake* published in *Navire d'Argent* (Paris)	Woolf, *Mrs Dalloway*; Yeats, *A Vision*; Kafka, *The Trial*; Eliot, "The Hollow Men"
1926	Much of *Ulysses* pirated serially in *Two Worlds Monthly* (New York)	General Strike in England; Pound, *Personae* (collected shorter poems)
1927	First of seventeen installments (by 1938) of *work in progress* published in *transition* (Paris) by Eugene Jolas	Lewis, *Time and Western Man*; Woolf, *To the Lighthouse*; Surrealism in France
1928	*Anna Livia Plurabelle* published in New York in book form in order to protect copyright	
1929	*Ulysse*, the French translation of *Ulysses*, published in February	
1930		International economic collapse; Pound, *A Draft of XXX Cantos*; Eliot, *Ash Wednesday*; Lewis, *The Apes of God*
1931	Joyce and Nora married "for testamentary reasons" in London on 4 July; death of John Joyce on 29 December	Woolf, *The Waves*
1932	Stephen James Joyce born on 15 February to Giorgio and Helen (Kastor Fleischmann) Joyce; mental breakdown suffered by Lucia Joyce, whose deepening schizophrenia will occupy Joyce through the rest of his life	

1933	*Ulysses* judged to be not pornographic by John M. Woolsey in New York, making possible an American publication	Hitler named Reichschancellor
1934	*Ulysses* published in New York by Random House	Italy invades Ethiopia; meeting of Mussolini and Hitler
1936	*Ulysses* published in England by Bodley Head	Spanish Civil War
1937		Picasso, *Guernica*; Stalin's purges in Moscow
1938		German troops enter Austria
1939	First bound copy of *Finnegans Wake* exhibited by Joyce on 2 February (not published officially until May by Faber in London, Viking in New York); upon declaration of war moves near Lucia's sanitarium at St. Gerand-le-Puy	German invasion of Poland on 1 September begins World War; Yeats, *Last Poems*
1940	Forced to leave France for Zurich without Lucia in mid-December	Fall of France; Battle of Britain
1941	Dies of perforated ulcer on 13 January, in Zurich	

Chapter 1

Introduction

I
Landmark: the ruined monument

When Wyndham Lewis attacked *Ulysses* in 1927, his appeared to be the most unlikely accusation: an excessive simplicity of mind. Forced underground by censors during its serial publication, smuggled out of France on pages folded into letters and parcels, freighted with those expectations of secret wisdom that attend a forbidden book, this was a cryptoclassic already before it was read, a subversive colossus; it could hardly fall to Lewis's charge that it had no ideas at all. Yet a critical description of *Ulysses* might well bear out Lewis's critique. Here is the story of the average sensual man, Leopold Bloom, whose middling fortunes in middle age remain ostensibly unchanged in the novel, which runs the short course of a single day. Canvasser for newspaper advertisements, he crosses paths with Stephen Dedalus, a 22-year-old who has already outlived his promise as Dublin's scholastic prodigy, whose career as artist remains wholly unrealized. Mr. Bloom rescues Stephen at the end of a day of debauchery, yet the quality and significance of their exchange is at best indeterminate. The older man returns in the end to the bed of his wife, Molly, whose (mostly) mute exchange with him does little to redeem the fact that she has entertained another man there during the day. If narrative generates and sustains the potential for meaning in a novel, if the plot is indeed the load-bearing element in the structure of significance, then it seems that Joyce has used a pennyworth of tale to hang a hundredweight of − well, of details, minutely recorded circumstances, but not those eventualities and changes that define the salient themes and values of a major work.

Does this judgment alter once Joyce's story reveals the logic and momentum of a shadow plot? The events of *Ulysses* run in parallel to the adventures in Homer's *Odyssey*, and the correspondences range from circumstantial details to the motives and aims of the protagonists. Leopold Bloom's wanderings through Dublin not only resemble the adventures of Odysseus (Ulysses) but also recall the destination and promise of that homeward voyage: the Greek hero's desired reunion with son and wife. The death of Bloom's son eleven years earlier supplies a rationale for his temporary adoption of Stephen, whose disaffection from his own father opens him to the paternalistic offices of Bloom; the husband's longstanding estrangement from Molly, initiated by the death of their infant, looks for relief, now, through the appearance of the substitute son. The *Odyssey* supplies *Ulysses* with a structural rhythm, but the narrative drive of the epic provides an energy in which Joyce's characters participate not at all consistently, for the most part not even consciously. That Joyce inscribes the crisis (and resolution) of his novel in the magic language of myth, in a kind of invisible ink, may conform to the general tendency of literary modernism to avoid direct statement. Yet many readers (especially *post*modern ones) will resist the premise that human experience reveals its meaning through external and typical patterns, and will require the father–son–wife relationship to be apprehended in ways internal and unique to the characters.

The oblique signification of the Odyssean theme in *Ulysses* defines at once its central, ramifying problem and the very problematic terms used to describe the status it enjoys in the history of the novel. A conventional account of the genesis of the novel tells of its emergence in the seventeenth and eighteenth centuries from a fusion of myth (fables, romances, moral allegories) and fact (diaries, journals, "news"). The two sides of the fact–myth equation seem to be exaggerated to equally extensive degrees in *Ulysses*. On one hand it is an encyclopedia of contemporary news, its myriad and timely detail attested by the need of Joyce scholars to consult those chronicles of current events, the several Dublin newspapers of and around 16 June 1904, to identify events and characters in the novel. On the other hand Joyce pushes the romance substructure of the novel into a radical form, recovering its deepest roots in the original epic quest of the *Odyssey*. To ask that these two planes meet

in perfect cohesion, so that each fact acquires an epic correla-
tion, is to prescribe an impossible ideal, one which nonetheless
describes a main direction of imaginative energy in the genre.
That the random matter-of-novel-fact might cleave to the
paradigms of ancient archetypes is no obscure object of desire;
to this limit of credible need the novel ever verges, if only
asymptotically. Yet the manifest experience in reading *Ulysses*
is that Joyce manipulates and confounds this conventional
expectation. He indulges and multiplies random detail increasingly over the course of the book, straining the sustaining frame
of the myth up to and through the breaking point. The ultimate
(absolute, final) novel, *Ulysses* enlarges each major feature
of its genre to dimensions hitherto unknown, but in doing so
voids the possibility of their reconciliation. It fractures the very
compact that provides for its conspicuous eminence.

This paradoxical achievement points toward the complexities
of Joyce's own moment in literary and cultural history, a
situation which, once apprehended, may suggest how his incen-
tives, far from perverse, sustain a rich and varied production
in his novel. "We must dislocate the language into meaning":
Mallarmé's adage applies to the generic as well as verbal
experiments of the modernists. They might revive and extend
a dying tradition by putting a reverse spin on its forms; by
writing against the grain of generic expectation. *The Waste
Land*, last of all pastoral elegies, occurs in a city; *The Cantos*,
supposedly the summation of lyric tradition, teems with the
anti-matter of chronicle, homily, and demotic talk. This disintegration of generic purity coincides with a reintegration that
includes new material, fresh possibilities.

A similar double rhythm compels the main lines of movement
in *Ulysses*. Its first six chapters establish the current state of
the art, reinforcing conventional expectations by applying
methods already well established in a contemporary practice as
varied as Henry James's, D. H. Lawrence's, Virginia Woolf's.
An apparently detached narrator enjoys linguistic sympathy
with Stephen and Bloom, so that the narrative fabric catches
up these protagonists as characters-in-voice, weaving the stuff
of their inner monologues into the background tapestry of

scene and event. No sooner is this careful synthesis perfected, however, than it unravels, in the seventh chapter, which uses its setting in a newspaper office to mimic the language and format of popular journalism. The inclusion of this extra-literary manner anticipates the range of styles exercised in the second half of the novel, where Joyce indulges a wild farrago of mannerisms: melodrama, satire, romance (harlequin), scholastic catechism, musical fugue, etc. Not all of these voices are in-compatible with the novel as genre, but in their variety and particularity they challenge and dissolve the tenability of a single generic method. In this way Joyce unmakes and remakes the conventional sensibility, opening new areas of awareness in the novel for writer and reader alike.

While these initiatives align Joyce with the timely enterprises of the modernists, his strategies also respond to a problem endemic to the form of the novel. It is more or less at the mid-point (after the tenth chapter) that he shifts into the high gear of stylistic exercise. In a conventional novel (speaking schematically), the half-way mark locates the moment at which the complications of situation and desire begin to move toward resolution. "Incidents and people that occurred at first for their own sake," E. M. Forster observes in his 1927 treatise *Aspects of the Novel*, "now have to contribute to the denoue-ment." It is at this junction, Forster complains, that "most novels do fail," for the variability of real characters must give way to the mechanical necessity of cause-and-effect sequence, of a narrative "logic" that "takes over the command from flesh and blood." Even though Forster's rather convention-bound account later faults *Ulysses* for its surplus of flesh and blood, he identifies a prime liability in the traditional plot-driven novel, a susceptibility that locates at once a negative incentive for Joyce's stylistic art and a rationale for its positive achievement. Sustaining his imitations and parodies through the second half of the novel, Joyce not only avoids the free fall of the narrative denouement; he erases any trace of headlong movement. Each chapter dilates into stylistic performance, shifting its source of energy from the linear continuum of plot or sequential events to language itself.

A sensibility as traditional as Forster's could hardly respond to these developments. Verbal constructs like Joyce's appeared merely as architectures of sound turning in a void. Joyce indulges his deliquescent mastery over language, or so the usual objection ran, in evident defiance of the novel's social ground, where story mimics history; where plot acquires its historical thickness. Marxist critics in particular have worried over Joyce's avoidance of the clearly defined story line, which marks the intersection, these critics maintain, between the author's imagination and the social reality that constitutes it. In his highly self-conscious medium of language, however, Joyce can be heard restaging the actions on which the stories of fiction conventionally turn. Interaction between people gives way to an exchange of styles; the reciprocating acts of characters reappear as a variorum of verbal mannerisms. This medley comprises the "heteroglossia" that Mikhail Bakhtin heard as the varied verbal stuff of a novel, where the socially and historically conditioned styles of an epoch are organized in a structured system, one which gives tongues to the whole socio-ideological economy of an age. While most novels require an effort to *over*hear a subtly graded modulation of idioms – their dissonance is often not even consciously intended – it is a mark of the generally colossal character of *Ulysses* that it presents its variable styles as oversize characters-in-voice. Gigantism is not a synonym for greatness, nor is the vocal record of a differentiated class structure the sole condition of importance. Yet the orchestration of styles in *Ulysses*, and the linguistic philosophy that attends this art, are the most conspicuous and suggestive facets of its achievement (these practices and attitudes provide the subject of chapter 3). The proximate source for this performance lay in Joyce's own earliest experience, for his ear was tuned in a vocal culture as complex and rich as the Irish society of his formative years.

II
Ireland and Europe: from the 1890s to the 1920s

W. B. Yeats has written:

The modern literature of Ireland, and indeed all that stir of thought that prepared for the Anglo-Irish war, began when Parnell fell from power in 1891. A disillusioned and embittered Ireland turned from parliamentary politics; an event was conceived, and the race began, as I think, to be troubled by that event's long gestation.

Yeats is surely correct in assigning to the absence of Charles Stewart Parnell an effect as momentous as his presence. An aristocratic landholder seeking reforms in the tenant laws, an English activist for Irish Home Rule, Parnell displayed a capacity for paradox that signaled his genuine ability to cross cultural barriers and forge useful alliances. To suggest that the hope stirred by his leadership in practical politics could divert itself after his death into the production of pure poetry, which served in turn to generate nothing less than the Irish Rising of Easter 1916, however, seems both to privilege the artists' distance from history and credit them with too direct a political force and effect. It is a literary conceit, at once wishful and exclusionary, for its longstanding acceptance has served to minimize the importance of actual social conditions in "that event's long gestation." It has also tended to reduce the historical content and political depth of Joyce's own imagination. The novelist's departure from Ireland in 1904 – exactly mid-way between Parnell's death and the 1916 Rising, in the depths of that political quietism that left Yeats's artists dreaming upon the bones of a new body politic – has encouraged commentators to write Joyce out of Irish social history; to deprive his work of its formative and enriching contexts. Yeats's romantic reconstruction needs to be examined, challenged and modified, in order to return Joyce's work to its historical ground, its first circumstances.

It is to the artists of the Celtic Revival that Yeats consigns the imaginative nurturing of Irish independence. Flourishing between 1880 and 1915, the Revivalists sought to recover the use of the Irish language, introducing it into the educational curriculum; they retrieved Irish folklore and songs for study, and established a national theater in Dublin to stage plays of strictly Irish provenance. They premised their efforts on the belief that political consequences would flow from cultural activity: Gaelic antiquity would provide the material source of ethnic identity, the stuff of national self-consciousness. The very terms of this claim – the political agency of literature is oblique – make it difficult to prove or refute. Yet the ongoing work of historical scholarship has shown that membership in the movement hardly constituted a cadre of proto-revolutionaries: suburban, upper middle class, often *Anglo*-Irish, many belonged to the very social order – indeed, the governmental caste – that a revolution would overthrow. Might some of these genteel partisans be pursuing politics by other means – using urgent but vague claims of political relevance to validate a romantic antiquarianism, a nostalgic taste for holidays in a past they never knew? The inspired inconsequence of much Revivalist politics can be heard in its characteristic literature, in the very textures of Douglas Hyde's poetry, which infuses the English language with a Gaelic syntax and so establishes *strangeness* as the standard and condition of beauty. It is the art of *l'étranger*, the Norman English writer, who turns the country he is occupying and dominating into the alien land – an imperial exoticism.

Joyce's initial resistance to this movement went to the issue of its (self-proclaimed) insularity, a parochialism that choked his already declared sense of membership in a pan-European literary community. That the political energies of the revivalists were leading them *away* from the society they claimed to be serving, however, was an irony to which he was fully sensible. The contrast between the Celtic delicacies of Hyde's Connaught and the Irish destitution of Dublin was proven by his own experience.

The fate of Joyce's family in the 1880s and 1890s gave him a social exposure at once exceptional and totally representative. The declining fortunes of his father led him from modest privilege through well-mannered poverty into near squalor; in little more than a decade he had crossed the social map of

Dublin. The lack of industry in the city accounted for the virtual absence of a secure working class and shaped the violently sharp divide between the two poles of his social experience – the affluent suburbs and the often astonishing destitution of its center. Here a surplus population of "general labourers," depending on casual or occasional work, filled the crumbling splendor of Georgian townhouses. Only one-quarter of the nearly 5400 tenement dwellings at the turn of the century was regarded (by the tolerant standards of the day) as structurally sound and fit for habitation; one-half was ever sliding into unfitness, and the remaining quarter had moved beyond the possibility of reclamation. Infant mortality and tuberculosis raised the death rate to 25 per 1000. Over this subworld the characters of a shabby gentility survived shakily. Shopkeepers, clerks, publicans, and their assistants seemed not to belong to a middle class in the English or European sense, rather to exist in a kind of space-between, affecting the manners of superiority, facing the possibility of collapse. Into this space John Joyce sank his family, forever harkening back to the patrician grandeur of the near past, constantly raising the specter of ruin in the future. It was, as it were, the psychic crossroads of the Dublin caste system.

Joyce's experience there structures his vision of the city and casts many of the characters the reader meets in *Ulysses*. The conventional working class – gardeners, plumbers, carpenters – has virtually no representatives here. Joyce's people belong almost exclusively to the lower middle class, often affecting a sense of superiority that is only a reflection of their own insecurity. Poised between upper-class aspirations and the possibility of descent through the no-safety-net floor of 1904 society, Joyce's characters inhabit a gap, a site of high anxiety in historical Dublin but, as recast on the pages of *Ulysses*, a stage for high verbal drama. This space-between locates a rich nexus, a kind of vortex point into and through which the various class dialects of the city come rushing. Joyce orchestrates this mixture – "dialogia" is Bakhtin's term for the practice – into his narrative with a skill as complex as the attitudes of a man who has suffered existence there. This rift in the social fabric also stands as an opening in the contemporary ideological construction of the world, a fault-line or fissure through which Joyce might see the dominant political convention of the moment for what it was, and a staging area for alternative possibilities, ideas of resistance. Two forces — mighty but for the most part unreconcilable — grew up in opposition to the situation left in Ireland by English colonialism: Irish nationalism, international socialism.

Nationalism and socialism had long stood in conflict on the Continent, but Irish history made their alignment especially difficult. The absence of a broadly based labor movement left the socialists fearing that a new Irish state would change only the flag, not the structure or values, of the existing society. Conversely, the trans-European culture of socialism threatened the ethnic and political identity the Irish nationalists were seeking to retrieve. The Irish Free State that emerged from the rebellion of 1916 and the ensuing conflicts would indeed sustain much of the class-structure and economic culture of the older order. But attempts to mediate the impasse between nationalism and socialism were not inconsequential: this debate focused much of the energy in the intellectual culture of Irish politics. Of the writers involved in the debate one of the most interesting is the socialist James Connolly, an intelligence whose developments between 1890 and 1916 (he was killed in the Rising) provide both a history-in-miniature of Irish social feeling and a parallel (ultimately a contrast) for the growth of Joyce's own political sensibility.

In "Socialism and Irish Nationalism" (1897), Connolly negotiates a strained settlement between his two claimants. "Even with his false reasoning," Connolly concedes, "the Irish nationalist ... is an agent for social regeneration," but only insofar as the patriot forces Ireland to separate from "the interests of a feudal [English] aristocracy." Nationalism, in other words, is merely an expedient for the goals of socialism, a catalyst to be consumed in the very process of class-revolt that it helps to stimulate. It is a tinder no less dangerous than it is volatile. "The arguments of the chauvinist nationalist," he worries, address those zones of atavism and barbarism, the alliances of tribe and race, that ever threaten a "national recreancy." At times, however, Connolly attaches his language of egalitarian values to a romantic and nostalgic nationalism, imputing to the "social structure of ancient Erin" a "form of that common property" that is collectivist. To locate a socialist millennium in Celtic antiquity is of course anachronistic, but the gesture points up the real problem of modern Irish history, in the rhetoric and consciousness of Connolly's avowed cause: he lacks any evidence of a working-class movement in the actual history of Ireland, past or present.

This absence defines an awareness central to Joyce's own youthful socialism, which grew from his early experience and crested in 1906–1907, in Rome, where his short-lived employment as a bank clerk coincided with a meeting of the international socialist congress. Among the rival factions at the congress he prefers the trades-unionists or Syndicalists, who subscribe to an anarchism Joyce justifies in view of the problems particular to Irish social history, in wording that forces to a focus the predicaments underlying Connolly's own argument and rhetoric. "The Irish proletariat is yet to be created" (*Letters* II, 187), Joyce knows, and this absence seems to warrant an anarchist program of change. A month earlier he has deliberated "the overthrow of the entire present social organisation" to force "the automatic emergence of the proletariat in trades-unions and guilds and the like" (*Letters* II, 174). These socialist goals also lead him, like Connolly, into an opportunistic tolerance of Irish nationalism, which would at least break the English-forged chains of a feudal peasantry (*Letters* II, 187). Yet he also suggests that an English presence would help to erase those most regrettable conditions in Ireland — serfs scratching at the land to which they are tied. For English investment would alleviate the shortage of industrial capital (*Letters* II, 187), a deficit that accounts for the absence of an organized working class (capitalism, according to one model of socialist history, defines a stage necessary to the evolution of the model State). Apparently paradoxical, in fact pragmatic, indeed ultra-socialist, Joyce's openness to the English also invokes the pan-national faith of socialism.

It allows him to endorse the hope, expressed at the conference, that the new century will witness the end of international war (*Letters* II, 174).

Seven years later came the crisis of socialist internationalism: the Great War of 1914–1918. On its verge Europe stood as a rickety collage of nation-states, adhering in systems of alliance that four centuries of diplomacy had evolved, bartered, and compromised. Four days in August brought the system to acute distress, plunging England and most of the Continent into total war. The swiftness with which social democratic parties capitulated to national war efforts – the Socialist Party in Germany eagerly voted war credits to that nation – may have dismayed socialist intellectuals like Lenin. But these developments forced fresh awarenesses on other Marxist ideologues; Henrik de Man, for example, saw that the claims of race and country operated far more powerfully than those of social class or millenarian cause. These circumstances and recognitions provide context and rationale for the Irish Rising and the development of Connolly's own revolutionary politics, which changed utterly between 1914 and 1916. Nearly global evidence convinced him that a nationalist and ethnic vocabulary, not words like *proletariat* or *aristocracy*, could define oppositions, force issues, tap political energy. "The time for *Ireland's* battle is now," he proclaims in January 1916, "the place for *Ireland's* battle is here." A month later the rhetoric is rising inevitably toward Easter: "no agency less potent than the red tide of war on *Irish* soil will ever be able to enable the *Irish* race to recover its self-respect" (emphases added).

Joyce also responds to those militant blandishments of nation and race. Does he dramatize his own susceptibilities in *A Portrait of the Artist as a Young Man*, when his counterpart envisions the Europe to which he is fleeing? Here Stephen Daedalus "raised his eyes towards the slowdrifting clouds, dappled and seaborne ... The Europe they had come from lay out there beyond the Irish Sea, Europe of strange tongues and valleyed and woodbegirt and citadelled and of entrenched and marshalled races" (*P*, 167). The prospect is no less timely than antique, for its constellation of fortress nations presents a vision of contemporary Europe in a nostalgic medievalism. But it exerts a devious appeal, identified and framed as such. The archaic diction and alluring music suggest that this romance of nationalism, like some of Stephen's other enthusiasms, is being displayed rather than professed by Joyce. Probably written before the outbreak of war, the words recover the urgency of a warning uttered as an oblique hortative, in the negative subjunctive of the imagination. Subsequent history confirmed the warning in a way that prompted greater directness. By 1919, when Joyce is writing the twelfth episode of *Ulysses*, nationalism finds its caricature-in-voice in the Irish "Citizen," identified as the Cyclops in the Odyssean parallel and stigmatized as the giant of monocular sight.

To be anti-nationalist, however, is not to be apolitical, and Joyce's rebuke should not be assimilated too easily to the longstanding view that his imagination is essentially untouched by political issues. His attention centers on a social covenant peculiar to the history of Leopold Bloom. Born in 1866 to a Hungarian father and Irish mother, Bloom enters life as a kind of dual national. In the same year Hungary initiated its rebirth as a nation, but with two allegiances: following the Austro-Prussian war (which began on 15–16 June 1866), it declared its independence from Austria, but it also accepted the Austrian emperor as a constitutional monarch. The Hungarian plan was put forward as a practical model for Ireland's relation to England by Arthur Griffith, in 1904, in *The Resurrection of Hungary*, and the contemporary oral culture of *Ulysses* takes cognizance of that. Bloom is rumored to be a member of Griffith's secret counsels. The casual comedy of Dublin political gossip has led commentators to diminish the credibility of this option, but wrongly, and it may recover some of its original appeal in view of the circumstances contemporary with Joyce's writing. To the fever of single-vision nationalism currently raging across Europe the Hungarian plan offers an antidote, encouraging a more pluralist outlook – a capacity and tolerance for doubleness. Already in 1907 Joyce expressed a similar aptitude in his readiness to accept English capital into a proto-socialist Ireland. But it is in the material of the novelist's art that these principles discover their relevance — or not; "technique," Ezra Pound insisted, "is the test of a man's sincerity." The very weave of disparate idioms that marks the dialogic achievement of *Ulysses* brings with it an endorsement of the values on which the Hungarian plan is based.

To posit this connection between aesthetic practice and political value is to bring Joyce into dangerous company. Modernists like Pound and Wyndham Lewis tended to articulate social beliefs in the language of art, often using literary authorship to endorse ideas of political authority. The claim of the romantic poet Shelley — "Poets are the unacknowledged legislators of the world" — exerts an appeal to which Joyce is not immune. His response to it evolves in a way that can be traced and compared summarily with the attitudes of other members of his generation.

The social potency of the literary imagination is a force that Joyce ratifies in his first attempt at his autobiographical novel, his 1904 essay "A Portrait of the Artist." Here the power he ascribes to the artist's Word — to incarnate the millennial State and race — breathes through the mythopoeic, ritualistic diction of his own prose:

To those multitudes not as yet in the wombs of humanity but surely engenderable there, he would give the word. Man and woman, out of you comes the nation that is to come, the lightning of your masses in travail; the competitive order is employed against itself, the aristocracies are supplanted; and amid the general paralysis of an insane society, the confederate will issues in action. (*P*, 265–266)

Ten years later Pound privileged his artists in "The New Sculpture," in lines that move to a finale strikingly reminiscent of Joyce's:

We turn back, we artists, to the powers of the air, to the djinns who were our allies aforetime, to the spirits of our ancestors. It is by them that we have ruled and shall rule, and by their connivance that we shall mount again into our hierarchy. The aristocracy of entail and of title has decayed, the aristocracy of commerce is decaying, the aristocracy of the arts is ready again for its service.

Both writers see the demise of traditional aristocracies, the self-consumption of the competitive or commercial class, and in that ruin the formation by artists of a new political order. But Pound could not have known Joyce's essay, which was rejected for publication (the two passages may stem from a common original in Nietzsche). The echoes nonetheless enclose an absolute difference in political philosophy. Pound's glorification of a hieratic priesthood, his esteem for ancient echelons of title and class, locate an authoritarian demeanor alien to Joyce. To that "aristocracy of the arts" Joyce would oppose "the confederate will." The difference leads him, first of all to a socialist politics, ultimately to a dialogic language that orchestrates differences, pluralities, tolerances. The state of Joyce's art differs radically from Pound's (or Lewis's), but their enterprises go to the single root of their joint historical condition. They are members of a generation compelled to reclaim the importance of literature in social as well as artistic terms.

III
Novel voices

When Joyce writes to Carlo Linati in September 1920, at a particularly high pitch of creative activity on *Ulysses*, he invokes a sense of tradition as the measure and value of his novel. Might these claims also disclose the more timely motives and aims of a modernist?

The character of Ulysses always fascinated me — even when a boy. Imagine, fifteen years ago I started writing it as a short story for *Dubliners*! For seven years I have been working at this book — blast it! It is also a sort of encyclopaedia. My intention is to transpose the myth *sub specie temporis nostri*. Each adventure (that is, every hour, every organ, every art being interconnected and interrelated in the structural scheme of the whole) should not only condition but even create its own technique.   (*Letters* I, 146−147)

The greatness of *Ulysses* appears to lie in its mastery of tradition, first of all in its refurbishing of a classical tale, ultimately in its perfection of novel form: its assimilation of encyclopedic detail to the underlying myth raises to a new order of magnitude those forces of fact and fable that fused (reputedly) at the origin of the genre. Yet exaggeration on this scale identifies a strongly anti-traditional energy in modernism. This is the temper of gigantistic parody – as the lines of classical portraiture swell suddenly for Wyndham Lewis, *circa* 1909, into proportions at once abstract, grotesque, wholly new. Mockery strikes close to the center of modernist greatness. Its colossi – *Ulysses*, Lewis's *Childermass* or *Apes of God*, Pound's *Cantos, The Waste Land* in its initial lyric sprawl (*He Do the Police in Different Voices*) – can be seen to rise not so much on a surplus of *original* energy as through hyper-awareness of the conventionalized nature of artistic expression, those rules which the artist simultaneously inflates and derides. Here is the ambivalent privilege of writing at a late stage of cultural history: the forms of tradition, firmly established, offer an opportunity for a negative apotheosis, a comedy that is at once destructive and creative.

Aesthetic self-consciousness like this is not exclusively modernist, of course. Its growth locates perhaps the main line of development in the history of the novel, and it points up a major relocation of value over the course of two centuries. The earliest novel criticism tended to stress only the moral implications of technique; Samuel Johnson accepts the emerging genre, but only as a means of ethical instruction, relegating its craft to a fashioning of moral exempla that will furnish "the most perfect idea of virtue ... that humanity can reach." These tenets endure well into the Victorian period, informing the practice of writers as various as Charles Dickens and George Eliot. By mid-century, however, a counter-current in the tradition is already rising: the aesthetic or art novel. In 1859, in *British Novelists and Their Styles*, David Masson confers the mantle of civil and literary authority, traditionally reserved for the poet-seer, on the novelist. While this sanction renews the moral mission of the novel, it also carries the demand that the verbal textures of fiction exact as much creative skill and critical attention as the language of poetry. Around this time Gustave Flaubert and Henry James are developing the principles and practice of the modern novel, less concerned with its moral function than its structure as an aesthetic creation. By the twentieth century the novels of early modernism — Marcel Proust's and Ford Madox Ford's before Joyce's — openly seek to lift from art the burden of demonstrating a moral truth, thus creating the conditions for free technical experimentation.

Linear, continuous, at least superficially "progressive," this standard history of the novel may scant the complexity of the tradition as a *total* legacy. *Ulysses* may be the last of all art novels, as the letter to Linati so forcefully indicates, but the same epistle points toward the moral gravity in Joyce's imagination, toward a thickening mixture of aesthetics and ethics in his achievement. The story of Ulysses that he knew "as a boy" is Charles Lamb's *Adventures of Ulysses* (1808), a text set for his intermediate examination in 1894 and a *locus classicus* of the moralizing convention in nineteenth-century literary culture. In this redaction Lamb reconceives the tale as a moral allegory, presenting Ulysses as a hero whose inner virtues are being tested and shaped in the crucible of experience. And so the relegation of Bloom's epic action to the interior sphere not only conforms to the "internalization of the quest motif" that characterizes most postromantic literature; it discovers at least the promise of a moral quest, a possibility Bloom seems to fulfill in the "equanimity" (17.2177) he attains in the face of Molly's infidelity. The very oblique angle to which Joyce tilts his moral discourse, however, entails a high degree of artifice, one which signals the dependence of his moral concerns on the values and practices of the art novel.

The double measure of moral fineness and aesthetic finesse is indeed a formative conceit in Joyce's works. In the 1906 letters to his prospective Dublin publisher Grant Richards, he characterizes the sequence of stories in *Dubliners* as a "*moral* history of my country" (*Letters* I, 62; emphasis added), but one that is told neither through direct statement nor in the indirect discourse of moral allegory. The moment of moral awareness comes instead when "the Irish people [have] one good look at themselves in my nicely polished looking-glass" (*Letters* I, 64). That a writer might secure his moral authority as a credible reflector, by a clear mirroring of contemporary circumstances, recalls a dominant attitude in late nineteenth-century realism. Joyce's emphasis on the *polish* of his looking-glass, however, suggests that his moral intensity is mainly a matter of artistic finish. Aesthetics are ethics, Wittgenstein would later claim; the practice of good writing offers a type and model of formal goodness (a conceit to which Oscar Wilde had given provocative testimony). It is not the lessons expressed in *Dubliners*, rather the razor-sharp quality of Joyce's verbal presentation, that will stand his audience at moral attention. The quality that determines *good* writing will develop and vary widely over Joyce's career − the exacting probities of his early naturalism will not last even through the rest of *Dubliners* (in 1906 several more stories remain to be written) − but the early statement to Richards locates Joyce's abiding faith in the moral responsibility of art, to art.

The ascendant values of Joyce's age will clearly lead to the production of a novel of art, and he displays the current state of the art in the overture to *Ulysses*. The first three episodes show the reader an exercise in a method familiar from, say, George Meredith's novel *The Egoist*: a lack of emphasis on plot, the development of separate but finely etched scenes, the use of interior monologue to center the presentation in the elusively intense consciousness of the protagonist − the "artist-type" Stephen Dedalus. The next three chapters shift into the domestic rites and duties of the Blooms, complementing their materialism with richly detailed naturalism and showing throughout the banality and compensatory fantasies of the *petit-bourgeois* couple; here Joyce conforms to the atmospheric conventions of recent French realistic narrative, Flaubert's *Madame Bovary* most recognizably. This process of appropriating and using up the offerings of contemporary convention serves at once to signal the timely mastery of Joyce's novel of art and, in a way characteristic of its true distinction, to bring this radical enterprise back to the very roots of its genre, to episode 7, to scenes of Dublin's daily newspaper − that repository of contemporary fact that supplies the novel with its nominal content, the news.

More than a generic in-joke drives this process, for Joyce advances the consciousness of episode 7 − and his novel −

into the medium of the daily press. Its windy stink — those engines of hot verbal air acquire the Homeric likeness of "Aeolus," god of the stiff breeze — blows through the inflated language of this chapter. Its layout also mimics a headline- and leader-format to frame a variety of short topical narratives. A collage of highly stylized presentations, "Aeolus" mirrors in small the shifting mannerisms of *Ulysses* — the exercise of style *qua* style first becomes noticeable in this chapter — and points to a formative model for this practice in the newspaper itself. Joyce's claim that "each adventure ... should not only condition but even create its own technique" recalls the discrete sectioning of contents and styles to sports pages, editorials, etc. And so the stylistic odyssey of the novel cycles back — no more oddly than seems appropriate to its fiction of the one *day* — into the conventions of the daily, of the quotidian, of *jour*nalism. On this circuit the consciousness of *Ulysses* continually travels, generating uncanny combinations of the extra-vulgar and the ultra-literary, the popular and the precious, the raw and the cooked.

The achievement came to Joyce with a difficulty that matches its importance. The tension between the Parnassian and public claims on his art is preserved in the difference between the two protagonists in *Ulysses*: Stephen Dedalus, an aesthete who has subscribed to the ascetics of medieval scholastic poetics, and Leopold Bloom, an advertising canvasser who purveys the language of conspicuous consumerism. However desirable their *rapprochement*, it should not obscure its own strenuousness, for it points up a generative tension in Joyce's development, in the evolution of his verbal art in particular, beginning in *Dubliners*.

In "Araby," the protagonist-speaker situates his language in relation to the oral culture of Dublin, which he typifies in images of the marketplace or bazaar. Here is the medley of demotic voices, the background sounds of history and variegated social class, from which the novelist (in Bakhtin's construction) draws his verbal stuff. Joyce's character passes through these environs with a manifest complexity of attitude — taking evident delight in describing so finely the voices he must censor out of his own curial speech:

On Saturday evenings when my aunt went marketing I had to go to carry some of the parcels. We walked through the flaring streets, jostled by drunken men and bargaining women, amid the curses of labourers, the shrill litanies of shop-boys who stood on guard by the barrels of pigs' cheeks, the nasal chanting of street-singers, who sang a *come-all-you* about O'Donovan Rossa, or a ballad about the troubles in our native land. These noises converged in a single sensation of life for me: I imagined that I bore my chalice safely through a throng of foes. Her name sprang to my lips at moments in strange prayers and praises which I myself did not understand. (*D*, 31)

The mixed feelings of fascination and revulsion may go to the divided state of Joyce's family, poised between poverty and gentility, and he elaborates this ambivalence in the more discursive textures of *Stephen Hero*, the novel he drafted (as the first version of *Portrait*) between 1904 and 1906. Here Stephen Daedalus is said to "read Skeat's *Etymological Dictionary* by the hour" (*SH*, 26), and his philological passions turn him away from contemporary usage, that hurly-burly of clashing class accents, into the vertical richness of words, the buried treasures of secret etymologies. Words "have a certain value in the literary tradition," he concludes, "and a certain value in the market-place – a debased value" (*SH*, 27). Yet Stephen's authority is forced, and self-contradictory, for he is deeply interested in words overheard "haphazard in the shops, on advertisements, in the mouths of the plodding public" (*SH*, 30). The naturalistic comprehensiveness of the novel extends to its character-in-voice, and the usually idiomatic narrative presents the varied speech of the city as its subsistence language, the ground on which the artist rears his verbal consciousness.

Stephen's contradictory attitudes to the language of the marketplace appear to be put on display by Joyce; to be contrived as one expression of the tensions he develops more explicitly and extensively in *Dubliners*. To its well-known chronological scheme – stories of childhood ("The Sisters," "An Encounter," "Araby") lead to accounts of adolescence ("The Boarding House," "After the Race," "Eveline"), in turn to records of maturity ("Clay," "Counterparts," "A Painful Case") and public life ("Ivy Day in the Committee Room," "A Mother," "Grace") – should be added another kind of developmental unity. This process consists, not of differences in the evident registers of youth and age (nothing could be more "maturely" relayed than the precisely observed surfaces of "The Sisters"), but in degrees of privacy; in the gradual wearing away of the individual's privileged usage and the increasing sway of an idiom recognizably, indeed conspicuously public: maturation of person is collectivization of voice. Apparently inevitable as a sociobiological fate, this process is also a fiction, a piece of artifice, one which Joyce constructs and exploits for expressive purposes.

A story Joyce wrote comparatively late in the process of composing *Dubliners*, "Two Gallants," responds to the aspirations for privileged privacy in "Araby." Placed in the adolescence phase of the sequence, "Two Gallants" complicates the tonal values of the earlier story: its protagonist explicitly fails the youth's desire for a purified speech, bringing this ambition to common ground in the language as spoke: "He spoke roughly in order to belie his air of gentility for his entry had been followed by a pause of talk" (*D*, 57). Thus "Two Gallants" talks back to the protagonist in "Araby," heckling the boy's attempt to resist the urging tongues of the marketplace, sweeping the curial music of his knightly romance into this fierce mesh – a weave of idioms alternately refined and raffish: "He felt better after having eaten than he had felt before, less weary of his life, less vanquished in spirit. He might yet be able to settle down in some snug corner and live happily if he could only come across some good simple-minded girl with a little of the ready" (*D*, 58).

The legitimacy of this art is at one with its bitter originality – it grew from the residual trauma of Joyce's own social experience. A dislocation of class identity helped to open the vocal register of his prose, but a feeling of lost dominance surely complicates the product. The regret that must attend such a loss accounts for a mixed motivation in this art, a sort of resisting reciprocity with the voices of parole. This generative tension extends into the project Joyce undertook immediately upon finishing the last story of *Dubliners*: the rewriting of *Stephen Hero* as *A Portrait of the Artist as a Young Man*.

In the new title Joyce was to lay preponderant emphasis on the last phrase, thus aligning Stephen with the youthful protagonists of the early stories in *Dubliners*, of "Araby" most suggestively. Equal stress should be placed on "Portrait": Stephen's proclivities as private romantic subject are framed, both displayed and distanced, within a narrative that exceeds him feelingly; that allows the varied circumstances of Irish culture and history to impinge upon his adamant declarations of artistic independence. Thus the mission he announces at the end of the novel represents a fusion of the personal and the collective – "to forge in the smithy of my soul the uncreated conscience of my race" (*P*, 253). Great hubris breathes here, of course; Stephen's rhetorical personality remains committed to the myth of the superior individual, the high aerial artist Daedalus. The trajectory of that faith aims him from the last page of the novel toward a career on the Continent – from which he will have returned, by the first page of *Ulysses*, as evidence (if not at first the willing witness) of the failure of such ambition. That circular plot bridges the fictions of the two novels, and if *Ulysses* goes on to dramatize the demise of Stephen as romantic subject, it extends the techniques of the earlier work, varying the practices used to depict the character's private life.

Chief among these is *musical technique*, the use of key phrases in refrain and incremental repetition. It is an invention fostered by the necessities of *Portrait*. Novel of education as well as art novel, it must allow the consciousness of its protagonist to develop in ways equally free and determined, combining an apparent naturalness of speech with a sense of artifice appropriate to the young artist's evolving temper. Musical technique meets these contrary needs. Uttered at the appropriate moments, the phrases acquire the immediacy and urgency of dramatic life; repeated like musical themes, the signal words comprise an aesthetic structure, which also deepens each utterance with a history of feeling, the emotions accumulated through the whole pattern (a strategy developed out of Joyce's early passion for Wagnerian opera, where leitmotifs repeat to similar effect). When Stephen enters Nighttown at the end of Chapter II, for example, a prostitute's lips "pressed upon his brain as upon his lips as though they were the vehicle of a vague speech; and between them he felt an unknown and timid pressure, darker than the swoon of sin, softer than sound or odour" (*P*, 101); the phrases and cadences that convey the delectation of falling reappear, like the memory of a pleasure suitably avenged, in Stephen's ascetic phase, in a penitential phantasm, where demons "moved in slow circles, circling closer and closer to enclose, to enclose, soft language issuing from their lips, their long swishing tails besmeared with stale shite" (*P*, 138).

Musical technique, as the term suggests, is an art of time. It signals a preoccupation with process, with temporality and sequence. The portrayal of "life by time" strikes E. M. Forster as the vision special to the novel (as opposed to the depiction of "life by values" in classical literature). Attention to the timely generates an art of the timeful, an emphasis on sequential plots (the "what happens next?" effect is assisted by the serialization of novels in progress). Temporal consciousness is already an acute awareness in Joyce's early fiction, one which unifies those otherwise disparate products: the developmental sequence of *Dubliners* and the five-phase architecture of *Portrait* tell the one story of "life by time."

If this vision of "life by time" is intrinsic to the novel as genre, *Ulysses* expands it in ways consistent with its landmark status. There are of course those local chronotopes, the meticulously clocked adventures of its eighteen chapters. Yet Joyce extends the temporal sensibility to far wider horizons. What Oswald Spengler calls the "ultrahistorical sense" of modernity turns its understanding of "now" upon a consciousness of "then" – a two-plane reality that Joyce reproduces by manipulating a parallel between present adventures and classical prototypes. Doubling Dublin through antiquity, he refashions the present as a site already crossed by time, already historical; its local details – like the coin Bloom has marked in hope of recovering it one day – already appear like the traces of ancient civilization. Not that the imagination of the novel moves through the emotional twilight of antiquarianism, the gloaming of learned nostalgia. The Homeric scheme is intensely problematical, and the gaps in the parallel may reveal more than the points of contact about the nature of the enterprise, to which we may now turn.

Chapter 2

Epic subjects

Epic and novel provide the double theme of George Lukács's *Theory of the Novel*. Analyzing the world-views special to the two genres, Lukács consigns them to distinct "historico-philosophical realities" and, in terms equally vatic and social-scientific, announces their ultimate irreconcilability. The confidence of epic lies in a sense of "the immanence of meaning in life," a condition that allows a representation of "the extensive totality of life." To this level of comprehensive significance the novelist aspires, Lukács concedes, but the old epic wholeness derives from an authority no longer available (a casualty of the post-Enlightenment era in which the novel originates). Whereas "epic gives form to a totality of life that is rounded from within," the "novel seeks, *by giving form*, to uncover and *construct* the concealed totality of life" (emphases added). In other words, the modern novelist must resort to schemes and designs of huge proportions in order to recover − merely to simulate, Lukács would contend − the sense of complete meaning that the epic poet enjoyed as the benefice of his cultural situation.

That Lukács began to compose his critical book in the same season that witnessed the beginning of Joyce's eight-year labor on *Ulysses* − the last spring before the Great War − is more than coincidence; it is context. If mass technological war is about to give the final lie to the nineteenth-century myth of progress through technology, if the utopian gaze will turn accordingly from the future to the past, then the nostalgia Lukács analyzes (and occasionally succumbs to) in his eloquent diagnosis is timely indeed. His warning about the delusive appeal of original or pure forms seems to speak directly to the imaginative desire of *Ulysses*, a modern novel that uses ancient epic as one of its principal structural devices. (This warning was indeed a prophecy, for the neoclassicism of the immediately postwar period includes an extraordinary number of major works and so identifies a prevailing need of that moment: André Gide's *Thésée*, Igor Stravinsky's *Oedipe* and *Apollon*, Pound's *Homage to Sextus Propertius*, Rilke's *Sonnets to Orpheus*, etc.) Further: Joyce's Homeric plan grows into the far more elaborate structure he describes in his 1920 letter to Linati, where he assigns distinctive symbols and technics to the episodes, and distinguishes these further by specific arts and colors and organs (full schema reproduced in the Appendix). In its variety and inclusiveness, in its use as a key to the "meaning" of the episodes (a Rosetta Stone Joyce cunningly created by burying it from public view for years), the scheme matches the designs that Lukács imputes to the modern novelist: this is Joyce's attempt to forge the kind of comprehensive significance proper to epic.

This project shows its ambition and likely fate through one of its schematic categories: human *organs*. Taken together, these form the basis of Joyce's claim to have written his "epic of two races (Israelite−Irish)" through "the cycle of the human body" (*Letters* I, 146). Assigning each organ to a place and metaphorical function in the city of Dublin, moreover, Joyce was also rewriting the old myth of the body politic. Image of essential union between private and public existence, individual members and the corporate *res*, the old figure of the civil corpus offers human society as the source and end of the individual's fullness of meaning. It promises that "extensive totality of significance" that Lukács invokes as the scope and privilege of epic − it depicts the kind of "organic" society he posits as "the only possible form of a rounded totality." Now, the innards Joyce displays with such Rabelaisian delight do participate in the essential life of some chapters: ear and eye certainly govern the channels of sensory awareness in "Sirens" and "Nausicaa," for example. But each chapter englobes its own organ, isolating and magnifying its sensory register, playing a kind of Jonsonian comedy of preponderant humors. The body (civil or individual) limned by these conceits appears merely as an aggregate of enlarged parts, the sum of those deformities. The exaggerations grow out of Joyce's refusal to subordinate the chosen organ to a larger organic wholeness; they provide evidence, writ very large, of the *in*organic, wholly mechanical character of the conception.

And so the last stages of the novelist's work on *Ulysses* seem to bear out a Lukácsian prognosis – in a manner at once grave and antic (its studious frenzy already intimated in the Linati letter). Joyce adds scrupulously voluminous detail to the text, increasing the size of some passages by multiples of four and five, using the schema of organs and colors and symbols to organize the surplus. The process shows a novelist straining to make his machinery achieve the completeness of epic, the plenitude of meaning that cannot, however, be artificed; that must be given as the condition, the cultural birthright, of the epic poet. The more detail Joyce generates and regulates, the closer he might seem to approach to the rounded totality of epic. The very modernity that compels this quest, however, has deprived him of Homer's organic order.

There may be an alternative order: not a structure but a self-regulating dynamic – a systematically mutating force, an energy that is at once forming and ordering and open-ended, in short, a language. So described, language functions like a social structure; indeed, *Ulysses* relocates the source of those common values (professed by epic) in the common language, a shift that will be followed through the next chapter. It is a process grounded in paradox, however, for a restoration to the language of the resources its speakers hold in common stems from needs sensed most acutely by individuals estranged from it – from James Joyce, whose command of a pan-European tongue positioned him at a most extreme angle of relation to his own, and from Stephen Dedalus and Leopold Bloom, who need for various reasons to consign their thoughts and feeling to the unpublic speech of inward monologue. These protagonists present in the marginal and alienated lives of private individuals a problem Joyce will resolve into a tonic concept of language, but their struggle works itself out most urgently, indeed primarily, in terms of the epic plot and the attendant values of a social community. A war of genres is joined here: against the promise of epic wholeness stand the protagonists of the novel, living the limited lives of individual subjects.

Stephen and Bloom present different but complementary forms of literary individualism, each of which brings its own fictional tradition. Stephen is the prime example of the romantic subject. To the challenge of public values in classical epic he responds through the ethic and convention of the *Künstlerroman*, the novel of artistic development, sampled most recently in *A Portrait of the Artist as a Young Man*, which portrays him as intensely, perhaps irretrievably, self-absorbed; his private imaginative and psychological experience stands as the one smithy from which great art can be "forged" (made, faked). Bloom's subjectivity stands as both source and symptom of his alienation from the social commerce of the Irish tribe. No less a factor in his estrangement than his Jewishness, however, is his "feminine" sensibility, a temperament Joyce cultivates in order to align him at once with the difficulties of women's political history and the literary tradition that springs from their alienation. A domestic subject, like the heroines in women's fiction of the late eighteenth and nineteenth centuries, he takes the state of social exile "inside" the house as condition and metaphor for the inner life.

If Bloom's inwardness serves ultimately as a staging area for alternative values, it works first of all as compensation for exclusion from the "outer" sphere of political activity, that is, from a position of deprivation. And so Joyce puts a fine point of Latin etymology on Bloom's — and Stephen's — status as "subjects": *sub-jectus* "tossed under"; in their differing ways they are both repressed, inferior, servile. The state of radical "subjectivity" in *Ulysses* goes to the roots of that word and returns a lesson and ethic of classical civics: fullness of value lies in the public place. How the two privacies of Stephen and Bloom interact with the social scope of epic thus defines the tension and main thematic in the following exposition, which may serve, among other things, to thicken the civic complexion of *Ulysses*: to contest the longstanding Marxist (post-Lukácsian) critique of Joyce's book as a monument to bourgeois privacies.

The organization of this chapter reflects the three-part, Homeric structure Joyce provides for his eighteen episodes: 3:12:3 (another division [9:9] will be applied in the next chapter, which examines the linguistic philosophy and stylistic odyssey). The Telemachia (1–3) features Stephen as the expectant son in the epic; the Odyssey (4–15) includes mainly the adventures of Bloom's day; the Nostos, or Return (16–18), reunites Odysseus and Telemachus in the developing acquaintance of Bloom and Stephen and culminates in the monologue-reminiscence of the Penelopean Molly, who returns to the scene of her first love for Bloom and, at least in memory, reclaims him. (Not that every chapter functions wholly or primarily in the furthering of the epic plot: some episodes reveal their main import in other critical contexts, and detailed discussion of these is accordingly deferred.)

The exposition that follows also divides Joyce's story into six units of three episodes each. A longstanding assumption of schematic critics – Richard Ellmann extends it furthest – maintains that Joyce organizes and sequences by threes; that he moves between opposite extremes in the first two parts of a triplet, then synthesizes in the third. These triads will serve here to organize the major phases of movement in *Ulysses*. Within these units I will use the Homeric correspondences to focus issues relevant to the rival claims of epic and novel, in order to define and test the kind of syntheses Joyce manages to achieve.

The ultimate trio is of course Stephen-Bloom-*Molly*. If she confirms *three* as the structural number of Joyce's imagination, one of her roles in the larger design of the book is to celebrate and extend reconciliations already won between novel and epic, between private and public values. For she shifts the secret things of the interior life into and through the autonomous force of language, a collective energy that sweeps the forbidden to disclosure and acceptance and so achieves the concords of high comedy (this is not to diminish the constant threat she presents to the moral decorum of any social status quo). No anomalous presence at the end of the book (as some readers have found), no surprise peripeteia, she consummates and

perfects the values to which *Ulysses* aspires, and her chapter
will be read in the end accordingly.

I
Telemachia
1–3
Shadowy possessions

The first tercet situates Stephen as "subject" in the full and
complex sense of that word. "Tossed under" the public *res*,
driven in on himself by a range of forces both personal and
social, he occupies his lonely individuality as a position of
inferiority, captivity, unfreedom. While Joyce historicizes and
politicizes this condition, reinforcing it as well through Homeric
identifications, the protagonist attempts to redeem the time,
and this counterrhythm carries a single energy through the first
three episodes.

In "Telemachus" (episode 1), Stephen appears as servant –
by turns silent and surly – to Buck Mulligan, a master who
stands in the place of Stephen-Telemachus's absent father (he
permits Stephen to live in the tower on which he pays rent).
Buck is also the "usurper" (1.744) of Stephen's legal patrimony,
the privileges and rights over the language that the young artist
feels is his due: verbally, Buck upstages Stephen at every point.
The wrongfulness of this dominance emerges in part through
its parallel to the English presence in Ireland. "Stately, plump
Buck Mulligan" (1.1): here is the poet-priest of the swollen
imperial State. Its network of local connection is sampled in the
company Buck keeps with the Englishman Haines (10.1043ff.),
the third tenant in the tower, and the facility of its power smiles
through the genial ease of his command, his jaunty verbal mien.
When colonization reaches the culture and language of a people,
the muses jangle, and Mulligan's jingles earn the laurel wreath.
"Four omnipotent sovereigns" (1.297), Buck exclaims like the
king's gleeman, here invoking English royalty to warrant his
plunder of Irish wealth, the pay Stephen will receive that day
for his teaching labors.

Imperial appropriation appears again through the figure of Haines. The only one in the tower to speak Irish (to the uncomprehending milkwoman), the Englishman represents that distinctly *Anglo*-Irish phenomenon, the Celtic Revival. He owns a silver cigarette case in which a green jewel is set (1.615–616) – image of the Emerald Isle fixed in the silver compass of British rule, it frames Ireland as artifact, knick-knack, aesthetic curio. It displays the mastery that drives the true artist into "silence, exile, and cunning" (*P*, 247), or so Stephen might have consoled himself on his way to the Continent earlier – but not now, for the condition of alienation and "quiet" (a word used repeatedly for Stephen in the tower) in one's own land loses its *glamour*, that is, its *grammar* (the words meet at the root). Virtually speechless in this tower of estrangement, Stephen reduces his dramatic talk to tersely gnomic rejoinders to the masters Mulligan and Haines. Otherwise turned inward, self-absorbed but hardly self-confident, he recovers the fully negative sense of *subject*ivity: shoved beneath the breath of inward monologue, his words move in a subjugation reckoned by its failure to participate in a public speech.

"It seems history is to blame" (1.649), or so goes Haines's lame apologia for the Irish predicament bearing everywhere on Stephen's own. Thus the rising action of engagement and conflict leads Stephen in episode 2 ("Nestor") to attempt to repossess "history" (the declared art of this chapter) and so to recover the full ground of a valid language, civil as well as literary. He contests the meaning of history with the Protestant-Irish proprietor of the academy in which he is teaching, Mr. Deasy, who resembles Nestor (in Book III of the *Odyssey*) in providing inadequate counsel to Stephen-Telemachus. Deasy nonetheless offers a going notion of history to ballast the young man's own. Deasy's scheme represents a compound of Darwinian evolution and biblical eschatology. "All human history moves towards one great goal," the bland psychopomp intones, "the manifestation of God" (2.380–381). It is a dreary prospect – not despite but because of its promise. To defer the meaning of the moment to some absolute, terminal, but infinitely postponable revelation is to endure a sagging interim –

minute by painful minute, fact by boring fact, one damn thing after another piles toward the ultimate, not-as-yet event. It entails (at best) patience, to be rewarded by the kind of slowly accruing financial investment that Deasy counsels Stephen to undertake. Where Homer's Nestor is the famed "tamer of horses," Deasy's attempt to break (what is left of) Stephen's spirit is signaled ominously by those "images of vanished horses" that bedeck his study, "their meek heads poised in air" (2.300–301). Here, however, Stephen will not yield; will not back into harness to plod step-by-step to Deasy's millennium. "That is God" (2.383), Stephen retorts, "A shout in the street" (2.386) – the goal of history is relocated in the joyous noise of boys scoring a goal in hockey.

Transposing the divine finale into the resplendent present, Stephen shifts meaning from imm*i*nence – what comes *next* (deferral is the rule) – to imm*a*nence: what lies *within*, a potential to be realized in any moment. He grants the artistic imagination both the task and the capacity to reveal what sequential time will not. He makes his case near the beginning of the chapter, as he ponders an alternative to the mere sequence of facts he is obliged to make his students recite in the history lesson: "A phrase, then, of impatience, thud of Blake's wings of excess. I hear the ruin of all space, shattered glass and toppling masonry, and time one livid final flame" (2.7–10). Despite the spectacle of time ending, Stephen is not endorsing Deasy's model of the divine finale. He has shifted the axis of time and the mode of its fulfillment from the exterior sphere of a collective history to the inner plane of the romantic – Blakean – imagination. Apocalypse is now private, a function of one's personal capacity for vision, its incandescent instant a potentially constant experience. This is all hefty compensation for the losses history has visited on the Irish artist. It is also dangerous recompense. For Stephen is reclaiming time in a mode that only replicates his condition as radical *subject*: an inward condition, an individual way of seeing, it stands surely as a diminished and inferior version of the public, world-history that Deasy presents with the assurance of imperial destiny (his march of time replicates and validates the spatial extensions of empire, which proceed ever with the sanction of providential fulfillment). "History to the defeated may say alas, but cannot help or pardon": the Darwinian morality of Auden's (later suppressed) poem, "Spain 1937," pertains all too well to Stephen as subject, at least for now.

This situation will have changed with the completion of Bloom's odyssey, at the end of episode 15. There the epic parallel turns the narrative toward home and extends promises of reunion, reconciliation, repossession; Bloom will reopen history to Stephen as private subject — a gift negotiated in terms special to Bloom's own fictional character, its valence established in the odyssey that provides substance for the second part of this chapter.

That meeting and its promises are already invoked in the last moment of episode 3 ("Proteus"), as the end and culmination of the Telemachia. Here Stephen's walk on the strand leads him to the imaginative prospect of the sea-sailing father's return, where the language of heraldry recurs in the archaic Norman phrasing (emphasized here); where the promise of Nostos, or Return, celebrated in a diction thick with the music of concord and reconciliation ("sails brailed"), ritualizes the phrasing, lifts the cadence toward incantation:

He turned his face over a shoulder, *rere regardant*. Moving through the air high spars of a threemaster, her sails brailed up on the cross-trees, homing, upstream, silently moving, a silent ship. (3.503–505)

The ship is the *Rosevean*, the reader learns in episodes 8 and 16, where its Odyssean resonances increase — only to grow increasingly troubled. It has brought a pseudo-Odysseus back to Ireland, a supposedly world-traveled seaman, D. B. Murphy, who is in fact a preposterously unconvincing yarnsman. The bogus character of the Odyssean father in "Eumaeus" already poses the question, in "Proteus," of the Telemachian son. Has Stephen earned the promise of paternity that Joyce's Homeric symbolism forces his language to celebrate?

If the father mediates the son's relation to society and so guarantees the boy's portion of the common wealth, then the language of "Proteus" is already animate with a supra-personal energy; it is as though the words were driven by an autonomous force, a collective resource opened by the very paternity promised at the end of the episode. Whereas the Greek hero Menelaus was strong enough to hold the sea-god Proteus lightly, thus to allow the god to change shape in his hands, Stephen relaxes his grasp on language in this episode (the linguistic rationale is discussed in chapter 3) sufficiently to free its own currents. These are collectivizing, anti-individualist forces, and as such carry the energy of the socializing father, for they run independent of the individual speaker and go counter to his claims, as isolated individual, on simple and single relations between words and things. There are no stable counters; objects are named in metaphors, by proximate likenesses, and these verbal figures constantly change the image of what is named. A cocklepicker's dog thus alters its shape through a virtual bestiary of fabulous comparisons: it "made off like a bounding hare ... trotted on twinkling shanks ... halted with stiff fore-hoofs ... reared up at them with mute bearish fawning ... loped off at a calf's gallop" (3.333–348).

Of these likenesses the most suggestive may be the dog's trot on "twinkling shanks," which causes Stephen to see "a buck, trippant, proper, unattired" on "a field *tenney*" (3.336–337; emphasis added) – the word for *tawny*, used specifically for that color on coats-of-arms. The image of heraldic blazon here focuses Stephen's abiding concern with paternity: a buck trippant, proper, unattired, recalls specifically the improper heir, Buck Mulligan, who also trips nimbly, especially when unattired for his morning swim. This verbal crux is also a crucial juncture, a nexus charged with rival values. The figure of the "proper" son taps into ideas of primogeniture, of the first (and only) son, of solitary possession, of the individual subject (son as subject to the father). To this customary attitude *Ulysses* will mount its most profound challenge, exchanging the natural or "legitimate" father Simon Dedalus for the adoptive *père* Leopold Bloom, whose status as Everyman figure serves, among other things, to multiply paternity across his inclusive character and so diversify the resources (like the linguistic powers released in this episode) handed on to his (second) son.

He overplays the father hand.

These values complicate any attempt to center the epic plot —
here the developing relation between Stephen as son to Bloom
as father — in the private intentions of integral subjects.
Not that critics have been ready to forgo the old standard of
individual primacy. A line of criticism stretching from F. R.
Leavis maintains that the several mythic possibilities of the
father–son bond — Odysseus–Telemachus, Noah–Japhet,
King Hamlet–Prince Hamlet — are released by a sheer
machinery of literary allusion and so reside entirely outside the
felt life of the individual characters, and thus remain invalid.
Insofar as Stephen shares residually in those values of privileged
privacy, so does his reader, whom Joyce consistently puts on
the spot — in the dubious position of one applying the Homeric
plot to the inner life of the modern characters by main
hermeneutic force. If the promise of sonship is richly endowed
by the Homeric titles for the book and episodes (used in the
schema and the original serial publications), it is realized in
the actual fabric of the character's emotional and verbal life
but, in these early episodes, no more urgently than suspiciously.
Consider the invitations Stephen's language extends as he
observes the midwives walking on the strand. "What has she
in the bag? A misbirth with a trailing navelcord, hushed in
ruddy wool" (3.36–37). What lies hushed in this *ruddy wool*
is a whispered invocation of Rudy, Bloom's dead infant son,
especially insofar as the wool anticipates the white lambkin
Bloom confers on the boy in the fantasy at the end of "Circe"
(15.4967). Yet the narrative context strongly resists this interpretation — Stephen has not even met Bloom, let alone imagined
himself a substitute son. Gratuitous but irresistible, these verbal
associations cannot be generated or controlled by Stephen's
conscious processes; the language moves his thoughts to ends he
knows not of, and so participates in the very socializing force
of the father–son bond that these words invoke. Coercion?
Gentle mentoring? The quality and significance of this force
may be assessed at the end of Bloom's odyssey, one of the
appreciations to be gained by following it.

II
The odyssey

Leopold Bloom is no less a subject than Stephen Dedalus, but the terms of his subjection differ from Stephen's. Bloom's condition turns on the loss of dominance in his own domus: Molly's sexual tryst with Blazes Boylan is scheduled to occur there at 4:00 p.m. Like Stephen, Bloom deals with this situation in a way that confirms his status as radical subject: repressed, driven in on himself, he enacts an internalized drama, one in which Boylan – too painful and odious a reality to be faced – hovers as an image and name on the edge of consciousness, a specter Bloom can neither forget nor, at first, address. This internal agon culminates in episodes 11 and 12, however, in a taking of decisive attitudes in public, and the sidelong fashion in which Bloom has dealt with his betrayal traces a subtle but central line of movement beneath the narrative. This gradual shifting from private to public enunciation acts out a main plot in Bloom's odyssey, a development that ratifies the main axis of value in Joyce's whole imaginative project: to rewrite novel into epic and so to reconcile the private subject with the larger civil *res*. The hidden moves into view in *Ulysses*, we shall see, in ways both gradual and sudden: as the macroplot of Bloom's odyssey and, spontaneously, in slips of the tongue, in local moments of self-revelation to others. These movements also participate in the energy of social comedy, where things formerly forbidden become known and (at least partially) accepted, and its rhythm rises through Bloom's day.

Does Joyce's comedy merely restore the old social hierarchy with an infusion of renewed male ego? Such dominance is always shadowed by subjection, so that a restoration in the end of the authoritarian male will only reverse the gender roles and revive the original problem. Joyce's sociological plot is linear, however, not circular; new states (of mind) are envisioned and attained. The uncertainty of Bloom's role in the domus – he is master *manqué* – opens the persona of heroism for reimagining, provides context and opportunity for diversifying its gender: Bloom's temperament shows a "feminine" element.

If this aspect of his character matches initially with his status as domestic subject, it leads him eventually out of social exile within the house and into public view — into balance with his male element in episode 12 and, shortly afterward, into position as double-gendered parent to Stephen. This process describes a social reconciliation that comprises but exceeds the aims of high comedy. For this dual gendering, its fulfillment of human potential and the civil possibilities that attend it, may realize the loftiest claims that Lukács imputes to epic, which "gives form to a *totality of life* that is *rounded from within.*" A review of the literature of the domestic subject and its bearing on the conception of epic contemporary with Joyce may thus lead to this reading of Bloom's odyssey.

The domestic emphasis of *Ulysses* reflects those tendencies of modern classical scholarship that Heinrich Schliemann advanced, in 1870, when he excavated Troy. The city that had existed for millennia on the mistiest peaks of myth suddenly came to ground; it became as real as its streets and sewers, as intimate as the relics of its quotidian life. These new awarenesses sound through the translation of the *Odyssey* that Samuel Butler published in 1900, which presented a civilization grounded in actualities — a milieu dense with familiar things, as well lived in as the phrases of Butler's own idiomatic prose. His translation followed naturally on his "scholarly" book, *The Authoress of the Odyssey* (1897), which argued that a woman had composed the poem and infused it with "female" values. Household deities thus supplant the gods of war and supernal fate as the abiding spirits of the poem, as Hugh Kenner constantly reminds Joycean archaeologists. Yet this shift in muse is also one of authorial gender, and it represents an internalization in a fully double sense. The imaginative focus moves from the exterior world of male action to the interior sphere of the female psyche.

Joyce owned a copy of this book, and its bearing on *Ulysses* is suggested in Butler's identification of crises closest to Bloom's own — crises that define for Butler the feminine sensibility of the *Odyssey*: illicit sexual affairs, the loss of a son. Thus the maidservants' commerce with the suitors receives a punishment in the *Odyssey* far fiercer, Butler points out, than the swift and sure retribution to be meted out by a male; its intensity measures the authoress's domestic morality and her character-istically "female" way of nurturing a grievance, growing in ferocity as it steeps. "Again, the fidelity with which people go on crying incessantly for a son who has been lost to them for twenty years," he continues, "is part and parcel of that jealousy for the sanctity of domestic life, in respect to which women are apt to be more exacting than men." These local affinities between Butler's *Odyssey* and Joyce's *Ulysses* point to a radiating influence, one which allows commentary on the epic parallels to exceed the merely this-for-that element in the Homeric correspondence; one which shows the formative force of this feminine temper. Here emotional preoccupation (verging on obsession in Bloom's case) replaces the efficacious deed as the center of attention; here diminishing interest in a linear narrative of action shows in a mounting complexity of verbal and psychological texture in local moments.

Yet Joyce's major extensions of Butler's initiative show in a field far less specialized than Homeric scholarship. Butler is rewriting the *Odyssey* as a nineteenth-century novel, and in doing so he summarizes and typifies the forces in social and intellectual history that compel the evolution of that genre. The rising political status of women was matched by a mounting prominence of the domestic interest in fiction, as Nancy Arm-strong has shown. Here qualities of mind rather than inherited status defined the merits of the heroine; ignoring the political world run by men, the literature of domestic women offered subtleties of temperament and demeanor as the stuff of real worth. By the end of *Jane Eyre* − to take the most obvious example − Rochester lays aside his aristocratic character, exchanging the old male echelon of title and class for a matrix of feeling dominated by a woman esteemed sheerly for her fineness of sensibility. The female who possessed psychological depth and a commensurate moral value utters her quiet but effective challenge to the male hierarchy she so subtly supplants. In the same way, Butler depicts his authoress sitting with the pages of the *Iliad* spread before her, methodically rewriting that narrative of active male heroism to stress those values of domestic morality and emotional intensity that are, for Butler, specifically feminine. Joyce continues the process in his casting of Bloom's character and its recasting of the traditional male role in epic. Yet Butler's rhetoric and conception remain tied to gender disparities that seem absolute: he sees distinctly and infrangibly male and female temperaments. Joyce's extension of this tradition will move to a view of gender roles as non-essential, as plastic or variable states of mind, as attitudes to be included in one full — fully and suitably complex — human temperament. For Bloom is "the new womanly man" (15.1798–1799).

If this dually gendered role represents the social reconciliation of high comedy, and as such the modern epic novelist's recovery of an extensive totality of significance, it is also — first of all — a state of mind (and body). Thus Joyce's epic subject still appears to be the refinement of Bloom's inward sensibility, the primary importance of which needs to be asserted here. Such internal emphasis was paramount in the first version of the epic that he encountered: that redaction by Charles Lamb, *The Adventures of Ulysses* (1808). Lamb's introduction presents the fable as an allegory of spirit, one in which Ulysses struggles through a process of testing and shaping that has distinctly moral overtones. Like Aeneas in medieval Latinity, like Beowulf through the monks' interpolations, Lamb's Ulysses is certainly imperfectly regenerated for Christian presentation. But even if Lamb's moral imagination works only momentarily, usually in a local or *ad hoc* way, it exerts a force that is more than merely rhetorical or decorative; it opens up the internal dimensions of the hero as the site of most significant action. Lamb's account is Joyce's first point of contact with the epic myth, and its emphasis on the importance of the internal event remains as his lasting apprehension of its hero.

A striking sign of this emphasis and its abiding influence appears in Lamb's version of the encounter in Hades between Ulysses and the prophet Tiresias. The seer must convey to the hero the news of the suitors in his hall − an episode that provides type and pattern for Bloom's day-long preoccupation with Boylan, who presents to Bloom's Odysseus the prime type of Antinous, hottest and noisiest suitor to Penelope. That Joyce's modern Odysseus cannot at first face this fact opens the whole process of evasion and coded recognition that will be followed later here, and this internal drama seems to have been scripted for the situation in which Lamb's Tiresias puts his Ulysses:

For Ulysses the gods had destined him from a king to become a beggar, and to perish by his own guests, unless he slew those who knew him not.
This prophecy, ambiguously delivered, was all that Tiresias was empowered to unfold ...

Whereas contemporary translations of the *Odyssey* − Butler's, and that more standard classical edification, the sables-and-diamonds version of S.H. Butcher and A. Lang (1879; rpt. 1900) − present this news as a straightforward matter of fact, Lamb's Tiresias dissembles, riddles, providing a cryptic and ambivalent report. It leaves Ulysses attempting to grapple with a fact he cannot face. Here indeed is prelude and prophecy of the inner turmoil of Bloom's own day. This whole agon represents a massive relocation of site and value and gender from the original epic, the permutations of which may now be followed through Bloom's odyssey.

4−6
"Met him what?"

Bloom appears initially as domestic subject in "Calypso" (episode 4), arranging Molly's breakfast things in prompt response to her imperious commands. This 8:00 a.m. setting times "Calypso" with "Telemachus" and, besides initiating the synchrony between episodes 1−3 and 4−6, repeats the theme of servitude. The other parallel for Bloom's situation is with Odysseus's captivity on Calypso's isle (Book V). Both captivities are immensely pleasurable, but Bloom's state of "effeminate bondage" − Lamb's phrase applies vividly to this domesticated husband and shows the lasting influence of Joyce's first encounter with the story – entails a *subject*ion altogether more complex, modern, paradoxical. Bloom's position inside the house clearly befits his condition as repressed subject, for he is wholly self-absorbed about the Boylan affair, but this inwardly turned energy will provide the force of self-knowledge and, in the end, steer him in the direction of renewed social relation. Thus the internal drama of recognition and admission that is staged first within the house, in "Calypso," moves with Bloom in the subsequent episodes into the social province of Dublin. This external dimension forces a constant surfacing of the hidden things and so compels developments from private to public, the main direction of value in Joyce's rewriting of novel as epic.

The first scene of Bloom's drama unfolds from the etymological meaning of *Calypso*: cup, enclosure, concealer. Calypso does not at first inform Odysseus that the gods have directed her to free him; under her pillow Molly tries to hide the letter from Boylan that Bloom has handed her, that arranges their meeting (Bloom manages to find out) for 4:00 p.m. His need to expose these would-be secrets likens him to the epic character, but the method of his adventure shows the psychological emphases intimated variously by Lamb and Butler. Mute, acquiescent, yet obsessed, he can face the fact of betrayal only inadvertently, in the form of a Freudian slip. "Met him what?" (4.336), he blurts out to Molly's request for elucidation of *metempsychosis*. That she will meet *him* – Boylan – is already known (4.312), but Bloom's awareness has no sooner been repressed than it is released, if in the self-protective form of this apparent mistake. The rhythm of disclosure is already rising, the repressed has returned and is turning outward for relief even now. At the start Joyce has established the main dynamic, a pattern both dramatic and thematic, for Bloom's odyssey of recognition.

Not that these energies of liberation proceed in automatic fashion. Release exists only in relation to oppression, and the double bind of avoidance and admission tightens in episode 5. "Lotus-eaters" occurs in the psychic space of the Lotus Island in Book XI of the *Odyssey*; there Odysseus's men fall into the pleasurable inertia induced by eating the lotus flower; Bloom lapses here into an anaesthetized state, yielding to his need to obscure awareness of the 4:00 p.m. meeting. The floral images that proliferate in the narrative here show a vegetal mind, a state of drugged distraction that signs itself as Henry Flower, the pseudonym under which Bloom conducts his covert correspondence with Martha Clifford and enters the sort of lugubrious make-believe that characterizes his several floral digressions. This evasiveness is countered by forces that work to disclose the subject, drawing forth things repressed by the private character and leading his obscure horror, ever more inexorably it seems, into public view. "Tiptop" (5.142), Bloom responds innocuously enough to Charlie M'Coy's inquiry after Molly. Rhyming doubly with "tup," the rural dialect word for animal copulation, these two syllables are loaded with covert meaning: the image of the tipster (Boylan shares his confidences about racing horses) topping Molly to tup her springs from the verbal foliage here (these sounds will mount to crescendo as the fated hour of 4:00 p.m. approaches, in the musicalized monologue of "Sirens"). Conjuring the scene of the inexpressible, Bloom is following the logic of dream, allowing the fears and desires that go unspoken in waking life to be released, here in verbal code.

That the psychological pressures at work here seek social disclosure, so to reconcile the private subject with the public view, may be attested by the fact that reminders about the secret start to come from outside, from the thickening matrix of Bloom's Dublin connections. "Who's getting it up?" (5.153), M'Coy asks blithely — about the singing tour being arranged for Molly, he now learns, by Boylan. The phrase reverberates to Boylan's secret tasks, a not so hidden meaning that obsesses Bloom sufficiently to prompt the memory of a song he overheard one night from a pair of prostitutes:

> *O, Mairy lost the pin of her drawers.*
> *She didn't know what to do*
> *To keep it up,*
> *To keep it up.*

It? Them. Such a bad headache. (5.281–285)

"To keep it up" then repeats as internal refrain (288, 292). The scarlet phrase enters first as a mistake — Bloom later corrects "it" to "them" — and shows the admission enjoined on him from outside conforming to the energy of errors like "Met him what?". Bloom makes the right mistake, it goes straight to his obsession, but he can express the unspeakable only on these slips of the tongue, which require a lapse of attention and so signal his inability to face the Boylan affair directly.

Bloom's deferred but unrelenting need to confront these secrets informs Joyce's sequencing of the Homeric plot in the next episode, too. "Hades" takes Bloom (and others in Paddy Dignam's funeral cortège) to the underworld (Glasnevin cemetery), the realm to which epic heroes traditionally descend in their search for hidden truths. Especially heavy reference to Homer and classical myth in this episode seems to weight it with the possibility of such major revelations. Here Joyce tells a version of Odysseus's meeting in Book XI with Tiresias, the seer who reveals to the hero the bitter news of a palace overrun now by suitors. Bloom sees the Tiresian revelation itself — Boylan, the rival suitor, his "spruce figure" (6.199) glimpsed as it is passed by the funeral cortège. It is a group sighting, moreover, and if the disclosure to social view of this previously hidden truth touches the thematic end of Bloomian revelation, the process is far from complete dramatically. The value of such disclosure hinges on its difficulty, after all, and Bloom's human resistance supplies his odyssey of recognition and admission with a tensility at once credible and necessary.

Thus Boylan appears to view — Bloom's, his companions', and the readers' — through an elaborate strategy of avoidance, a dramatic double-take that Joyce mimics masterfully in this ultra-elliptical method of presenting the nemesis:

He's coming in the afternoon. Her songs.
Plasto's. Sir Philip Crampton's memorial fountain bust. Who was he?
— How do you do? Martin Cunningham said, raising his palm to his brow in salute.
— He doesn't see us, Mr Power said. Yes, he does. How do you do?

— Who? Mr Dedalus asked.

— Blazes Boylan, Mr Power said. There he is airing his quiff.

Just that moment I was thinking.

Mr Dedalus bent across to salute. From the door of the Red Bank the white disc of a straw hat flashed reply: spruce figure: passed.   (6.190—199)

"He's coming in the afternoon. Her songs" are thoughts that precede the appearance of Boylan: "Just that moment I was thinking" of that interloper, Bloom muses ruefully, when the bounder appeared (in front of the shop that sells oysters, the food that promises powerful sexual performance). The apparent coincidence of Boylan's arrival at this instant points up the real possession of the protagonist's mind by his rival. It is the inevitable surprise: the logic of the necessary accident or Freudian slip compels narrative events as well as the character's speech. As in "Lotus-eaters," then, the landscape in "Hades" responds like Bloom's own consciousness, uttering the repressed name of Boylan in the form of that character's appearance. The avoidance that deflects Bloom's recognition into mistakes like the Freudian slip insures that his speech and the action surrounding it will remain charged with the force of the repressed, a potent locus of the expected surprise. The psychic inside turns into the social outside, an inversion that signals Joyce's major attempt to rewrite novel as epic; to work the private subject back into the public landscape.

The concomitant process in the restoration of Bloom's social relation is the recovery of the son, and the other sight he catches on the way to Glasnevin focuses this adventure in the epic plot: he sees Stephen Dedalus ascend from the strand (6.36—40) and his thoughts about his own child are reinforced and reoriented by the appearance of this other son. While Simon Dedalus's apparent loss of Stephen to the devices of Buck Mulligan (6.49—68) rhymes with the death of Rudy (6.74—79), the absences suffered by the two men open up one imaginative possibility: Bloom's adoption of Stephen. Renewed paternity is no less elusive or difficult a motif for Bloom than his awareness of Boylan, and it emerges, accordingly, through an equally elliptical method of presentation. Stephen's appearance to him as a "lithe young man, clad in mourning, a wide hat" (6.39–40) is thus mirrored obliquely in the fantasy it stirs of Rudy "Walking beside Molly in an Eton suit. My son" (6.76). The wish is more articulate, Stephen's presence in it more extensive: "If little Rudy had lived. See him grow up. Hear his *voice* in the house ... Me in his *eyes*" (6.75–76; emphases added), Bloom muses, and so catches up the images Stephen has used to affirm the fact of Simon Dedalus's (merely) biological paternity, a fatherhood *manqué*: "the man with my voice and my eyes" (3.45–46).

While Bloom can hardly be aware that he echoes the words Stephen utters to disclaim his father, his own urge to reclaim paternity through Stephen is no less valid. A critic's refusal to credit this process — Leavis's disallowing the Homeric scheme on account of a character's failure to express overtly filial or paternal feelings — stems from a hyper-valuation of the character as private subject, as source or intentional center of the meaning of his experience. It is to challenge and modify such fictions of self-sufficiency that the energies of Joyce's considerable artifice in these first two trios have labored: Stephen has moved from gnomic isolation in the tower to an enlivening participation with language as a force manifestly outside his control; Bloom's secret horror has been going irrepressibly public. And so these two protagonists are being swept together by energies independent of their own designs.

Thus the simultaneous narratives of episodes 1–3 and 4–6 seem to bring the two protagonists to positions from which they must seek out one another with a force as irreversible as gravity. Bloom and Stephen now cease to work in counterpoint; their concerns begin to merge and to compel them toward their fated union in "Circe": the first six chapters have set up a situation from which the Homeric plot will reach its conclusion reflexively, or so the line of argument goes among schematic critics, most notably Richard Ellmann. But wait, says Joyce's art of delay: the first four hours of this eighteen-hour day have taken (in each of the opening tercets) only one-fifteenth of the total page space; through the rest of the novel the only thing to happen precipitously is the dropping of the pace.

Non enim excursus hic eius, sed opus ipse est: "this is no digression from the thing," Pliny protests in the sixth epistle of his fifth book, "but the work itself." No less essential, Joyce's art of delay calls for an intermission.

On delay *But delay is the [writing] of fiction & not only Joyce's*

The slowing pace of *Ulysses* occurs mainly and increasingly as a function of Joyce's stylistic exercises. Literary, non-literary, and para-literary mannerisms are indulged in ever greater disproportion to the interests of an advancing narrative, not by sheer deliquescence, but, among other ends, to let the events of the fiction slacken comically off a normative or expected pace. Expanding exponentially through the second half of the book, the stylizing slowdown occurs already in episodes 7 and 9, at least in momentary or partial ways, so that the rhythm of the Homeric plot rising through the first six episodes is already checked at its first major station. These verbal practices reveal linguistic attitudes that await sustained consideration in the next chapter, but Joyce's art bears as well on the quality and significance of the epic story, as retold. Must *Ulysses* detain the progress of the *Odyssey* in order to retain the Homeric plot and, if so, why? A key to the motives and aims of Joycean delay lies in the novel that stands as the proximate, colossal model for procrastination. *Sterne*

In *The Life and Opinions of Tristram Shandy* Laurence Sterne concocts the most preposterous example of the story ever waiting to happen. An autobiography that purports to tell the tale of its author's life *ab ovo*, its first volume ends twenty-three years before his birth, its seventh and last five years before. The prankishness of the compulsive digression combines its humor with a searching critique of the very material culture that creates the expectations Sterne is confounding through his inveterate detours and backtracking: namely, the culture of books, the medium of print, which imposes its linear and sequential mode as a paradigm of progressive reasoning, of consecutive happenings. One thing after another, the apparently militant continuum of print presents a fallacy or paradox that

Sterne penetrates and dramatizes with comic genius. His insights anticipate the premises of some post-structuralist linguistics, in particular the Derridean concept of deferral or *différance*. Here the serial arrangement of language on the page projects meaning as a destination ever awaited but constantly withheld, and this interval space locates the primary place for the actions of reading and writing. Thus the digression, veering off the single track that print projects as its one axis of happening, captures the true experience of *litera*ture, of written *letters*, of books like Sterne's:

Digressions, incontestably, are the sunshine; – they are the life, the soul of reading; – take them out of this book for instance, – you might as well take the book along with them; – one cold eternal winter would reign in every page of it; restore them to the writer; – he steps forth like a bridegroom, – bids All hail; brings in variety, and forbids the appetite to fail.

The image of the bridegroom stepping forth to consummation provides the ultimate prospect of fulfillment, but here appetite is satisfied through deferral, the *via negativa* of print.

If deferral goes straight to the experience of reading and writing, the history of the novel is bound up with the culture of print in a way that establishes serial momentum-cum-postponement as the rhythm essential to the genre (a pattern institutionalized in the weekly or monthly serialization of many eighteenth- and nineteenth-century novels, a convention reenacted, at least to episode 13, by *Ulysses*). Joyce deploys this strategy at the most apposite moment in *Ulysses*, retarding the progress of his narrative just when the pace is expected to pick up, but his aims reach toward the ends of his special enterprise of epic recovery.

The possibility turns on issues relevant to the separate cultures of book and voice, novel and epic. Whereas the medium of print and the attendant effects of serial delay are natural to the novel, the oral culture that provides the originating circumstances of *epos* establishes simultaneity and presence as the rule of awareness. "The extensive totality of significance" that Lukács finds and esteems in epic may be considered as a function of this vocal simultaneity; song proceeds to no distant end, as projected by line or page or volume of print, but flourishes in its own resplendent, sensuous present. The sense of a synchronous whole in epic is created and reinforced by the poet's famed entry at the outset *in medias res*, so that the narrative moves by allusion and juxtaposition both "backward" and "forward," all in all canceling the sense of single linear progression and creating the impression of one massive simultaneous action. Such action is necessarily temporalized in the linear continuum of Joyce's page-bound writing, but why exaggerate the loss of momentum?

To defer is to enhance the valence of what is deferred, and the detaining of the pace in the novel not only serves to raise the value of the epic destination it approaches so slowly; Joyce reenacts the old plot, it seems, in another temporal dimension, altering its sequence to that of the dream time. The *Odyssey* may be reclaimed by *Ulysses* in a way that asserts its absolute difference from Joyce's present yet locates, in that space, its very appeal and relevance. The magical otherness of the *Odyssey* emerges in *Ulysses* through the condition of print, the order of books, the medium of the novel, which continues to defer the Nostos and detain the pace of the expected closure. We never really "get there," the reunion of Bloom and Molly remains as problematic as Bloom's fatherhood to Stephen is incomplete, but interest and value shift accordingly to the process of "getting there," to the waiting endemic to print. This interval situation is equivalent, in the thematic fiction of *Ulysses*, with the way private subjects resist – both complicate and enrich – the public values of epic. From the seventh episode, then, the arcs of movement in *Ulysses* swing longer. This lengthening of local temporal horizon matches the effects of deferral that are magnified from this point in *Ulysses*, beginning with the action of the next triplet.

7–9
"Almosting it"

These three episodes culminate in the near-meeting of Stephen and Bloom on the steps of the National Library (9.1197–1211).

The action begins in the offices of the *Daily Telegraph* newspaper, a source of verbal afflatus that occasions a parallel with the Homeric episode of the wind-god, Aeolus, whose gift of a bundle of breezes *almost* allowed Odysseus to reach Ithaca (his men disobeyed the god, opened the bag just as the ship was approaching home, and were blown off course). "Almosting it" (Stephen's protean phrasing, 3.366–367) appears indeed as an integral conceit in these three chapters. In "Aeolus" the narrative teems with evidence and legends of goals not quite attained: there is J. J. O'Molloy, who has reached the junior bar but failed to fulfill the promise of his youth; references to Parnell, who led the Irish people to the brink of Home Rule, gain resonance through allusions to Moses, whose death left the Israelites at the edge of the Promised Land; and Bloom keeps failing to secure his sure thing, his ad for the House of Keyes. Frustration also cadences the movements in the lunchtime chapter, "Lestrygonians," where Bloom pauses before several restaurants and almost eats several times. Tasting his hunger, he laces the landscape with images of food, the giving of which only famishes the craving. Disappointment then attends the reception of the much-advertised lecture Stephen offers the literati in the National Library, in "Scylla and Charybdis," which proceeds accordingly to his meeting *manqué* with Bloom at the end of the chapter. If these long-awaited non-events read like the promissory notes of Shandy, or as the ironic triumph of Deasy's myth of divine time, the absence of closure goes to the whole issue of the fit between Joyce's narrative and the Homeric schema. This question can be asked most searchingly of the final scene between Stephen and Bloom, which posits one destination for the epic narrative, after a review of Bloom's situation in "Lestrygonians," where he continues his agon of recognition. (Neither Bloom nor Stephen appears as controlling consciousness in "Aeolus," which is better considered in the next chapter. The shifting of verbal consciousness from those private individuals to the public forum of the newspaper is relevant to the socializing force of the father–son bond, but it may reveal its full import in the stylistic odyssey of the novel.)

"This is the very worst hour of the day" (8.494), Bloom complains at lunch-time; his search for the right place to eat lengthens into a mood of anxious but blank fatigue. His bodily determination for food suspends his thoughts and distracts his mind, letting down his guard and opening him to ever more pressing intimations of the worst *event* of the day. Not that he addresses his nemesis squarely. When Boylan appears at the end of the chapter (8.1168ff.), Bloom actually flees, darting into the covert of the National Museum. He is playing his now familiar game of resistance as recognition, and its psychology is acted out with suitable complexity and subtlety in the signal episode of the chapter.

The central scene of "Lestrygonians" represents a recasting of the original Homeric adventure, in Book X, where Odysseus's men meet the cannibals. Bloom, turning into Burton's restaurant, enters an equally savage prospect (8.650ff.), where the forbidden practices of Homer's tribe are centered in the eating of meat: "pungent meatjuice" (651) is Bloom's first and lasting impression. Carnivorism is hardly cannibalism, however, and the logic of the Bloomian substitution is given in the litany he chants over this prospect. "Men, men, men" (8.653): if red-blooded men (used to) eat meat, the supplanting of Bloom's own virility by Boylan causes him to bestialize this scene of flesh-eaters. The same logic informs his choice of an alternative lunch at Davy Byrne's "moral pub" (732): " – A cheese sandwich, then. Gorgonzola, have you?" (764). If the mythological Gorgon turned her beholders to stone, Bloom's naming of this food signals a need not only to substitute cheese for meat but to deflect his (verbal) gaze. Notice how the cadence and stress-pattern of Gor-gon–zo-la matches exactly with that of Blaz-es–Boy-lan (that unspeakable name discovers a small thesaurus of sound-alike phrases, to be heard in chapter 3); in fact, he has just been reminded of his rival as the barman asks " – Wife well?" (8.763). Responding to that question, he gives his lunch order: he puts Blazes Boylan's name in his mouth, in substitute syllables, in his very attempt to substitute cheese for the flesh on which that savage feeds. In line with the underlying logic of repression as involuntary disclosure, then,

Bloom summons the awful but unignorable fact by alternate words. Thus the private subject continues to conceal the forbidden truth he seems equally compelled to reveal to public view.

This process of dis-closure, an opening of private subject onto public ground, occurs centrally in the bonding of Bloom and Stephen in the roles of epic father and son. This process and its attendant values may be discerned especially at the end of the ninth episode, where Stephen first sights Bloom. The event emerges through an intricate and idiosyncratic art, one which reflects the developing interests of Stephen's own near chapter-length disquisition on Shakespeare.

Centering Stephen's attention is the paternal–filial imagination of *Hamlet*. That Shakespeare wrote the play just after his own father died, Stephen argues, makes fatherhood no less urgent a motif than sonship; Shakespeare creates Ham*l*et, Stephen goes on to maintain, as type and double for his own son, Ham*n*et, who died as a boy. Thus Stephen rises to his highest poetry in describing Shakespeare's fashioning of a son out of words; his reconstitution of fatherhood, now that flesh is gone, as literary creation. "The corpse of John Shakespeare," William's father, "does not walk the night. From hour to hour it rots and rots. He rests, disarmed of fatherhood, having devised that mystical estate upon his son" (9.833–836). "That mystical estate" appears as a quasi-divine privilege and power, in the celebratory language of the ensuing lines, when Stephen adapts the formulas of the Apostle's Creed. Here he implies forcefully that the work of the verbal imagination, Hamlet as *created* character, is the word-made flesh; the literary artifact is the only-begotten son: "Fatherhood, in the sense of conscious begetting, is unknown to man. It is a mystical estate, an apostolic succession, from only begetter to only begotten" (9.837–839). And the sense of mystery that Stephen attaches to this kind of imaginative procreation certainly attends his own brush with Bloom at the end of the chapter:

About to pass through the doorway, feeling one behind, he stood aside.
Part. The moment is now. Where then? If Socrates leave his house

today, if Judas go forth tonight? Why? That lies in space which I in time must come to, ineluctably.

My will: his will that fronts me. Seas between.

A man passed out between them, bowing, greeting.

(9.1197–1203)

The older man, sensed at first from behind as an unseen presence, almost preternaturally, passes between Stephen and Mulligan as an intimation now realized, as a hint or wish shifting from potentiality into reality; he moves from imagination into presence, from private desire into public demonstration. And so Bloom's appearance conforms to the rules of artistic creation, to the needs and laws of mystical kinship that Stephen has expostulated in the lecture – and to the direction of values in Joyce's epic novel.

Bloom also assumes the role of Odysseus-*père* in this final vignette. "Seas between": in this space the canvasser is not only sailing between the Scyllan rock and Charybdian whirlpool; he is returning as mythic father to reject the usurper or bogus son Mulligan, for whom Stephen's growing disaffection has now hardened into a resolve to leave the tower. In this climactic scene, then, Bloom appears to move simultaneously as mystical father and epic hero; as the projection of Stephen's subjective and artistic vision of paternity and as the public hero Odysseus, returning to cleanse a rotten house and society. Thus the Odyssean Bloom fits the private intensities of Stephen just well enough to pull the young artist in his wake, toward their narrative union in "Circe" and the social grounding Joyce will establish there for their relation. Such public valuation turns on the mythic father's own social status, which he proceeds to reclaim, in terms all his (and Joyce's) own, in this next tercet.

10–12
Facing the music

At 4:00 p.m., in episode 11 ("Sirens"), Bloom sees Boylan's car parked in front of the Ormond bar; surprised to find that the rendezvous with Molly has not kept to schedule, perhaps hoping to outwait it, he enters the lounge and, from a covert,

Boylan as nemesis is a bit strong given Bloom's guilt & ambivalence.

52   ULYSSES

beholds his rival. A protected recognition, a sheltered acknowledgment: this positioning depicts Bloom's characteristic way of hiding from the fact he is trying to face, but it leads here to something more than avoidance. Centering his attention, absorbing the presence of his nemesis and the truth of his situation, he moves through a drama of recognition to awareness of a new kind: admission of the fact leads to self-possession, an attitude and bearing manifest strikingly in the next episode ("Cyclops"), where he exhibits a newly resolute behavior among others. Shifting from private disquiet toward public composure, Bloom reenacts and extends the movements followed through his first triad, thus reaffirming that direction as the main axis of value in his (and Stephen's) book. The struggle and triumph of these two chapters provide occasion for major technical inventions, which extend leading motifs in the Homeric scenes Joyce is paralleling here. (The preceding episode, "Wandering Rocks," does not figure into this process; rather than focusing on Bloom, its detached narrative comprises all of Dublin, and its structural significance is best assessed at the end of this chapter.)

In Book XII Odysseus tells how he navigated the perils of the Sirens' Island, whose musical lure drew sailors onto their reef; eager to experience the seduction himself, taking care not to yield to it, he has himself bound to the mast, stopped his sailors' ears with wax, and ordered them to ignore his imprecations and row on. Accordingly, the verbal fabric of Joyce's chapter witnesses a musication of language, a conversion of words into acoustic tokens. This development represents a milestone and turning point in the sequence of styles in *Ulysses*, and will be read accordingly later, but it is important not to miss its first ground and primary rationale in Bloom's own odyssey. Here he faces the music, confronts his nemesis Boylan, but only through music; the betrayal becomes acoustic material, foresuffered and foretold as Bloom repeats a series of words and syllables (introduced in the overture) that resonate to the fact but, like music, remain inside a code. Like the mast-bound Odysseus, he can undergo the experience of the song without wrecking on the rocks of hard fact. Rising to a crescendo that is also an emotional climacteric, these loaded sounds — the car approaching 7 Eccles Street, the knock on the door, the bedsprings — discharge Bloom's debt to recognition, pressuring that awareness on him in a language at once indirect and unmistakable:

> Jingle jaunty jingle. (11.245)
> With patience Lenehan waited for Boylan with impatience, for jinglejaunty blazes boy. (289–290)
> Jingle jaunted by the curb and stopped. (330)
> One rapped on a door, one tapped with a knock, did he knock Paul de Kock with a loud proud knocker with a cock carracarracarra cock. Cockcock. (986–988)

That this music whispers the secrets of the self is attested by Bloom's parabolic science of the sea-shell, his analysis of that hoarse roar. "The sea they think they hear," he muses, but it is their own vital sound: "the blood it is" (11.945).

Listening to oneself through music is a process Bloom undergoes most demonstrably in hearing "The Croppy Boy," a ballad of betrayal and the loss of a family's male line (11.991ff.). Echoing the song in paraphrase, Bloom's response attunes its themes to his own situation:

> All gone. All fallen. At the siege of Ross his father, at Gorey all his brothers fell. To Wexford, we are the boys of Wexford, he would. Last of his name and race.
> I too. Last of my race. Milly young student. Well, my fault perhaps. No son. Rudy. Too late now. Or if not? If not? If still?
> He bore no hate. (11.1063–1068)

The recognition enjoined on Bloom by the ballad is also efficacious, stirring an urge to reclaim paternity. Its consequences are told in this chapter in terms of the Homeric adaptation, which allows Bloom to take up the role of Stephen's substitute father. This high note of imaginative possibility is raised as the names of *Si*mon Dedalus and L*eopold* Bloom are compounded (in response to an aria sung from the finale of the opera *Martha*):

> — *To me!*
> Siopold!
> Consumed. (11.751–753)

This consummation-in-advance of Joyce's Homeric plot, however, seems to sustain Leavis's critique all too well: here the epic
promise seems to have jumped way ahead of the protagonist's
declared awarenesses; Bloom has not even heard "The Croppy
Boy" yet, let alone intimated his wish to renew his lineage.
Objections of this kind retain allegiance to the self-sufficiency
of an individual character's feeling, the primacy of the private
subject's emotional intent and control. A greater power moves
through music, one that is consonant with the force of language
as collective resource, and this current leads fittingly here to a
proclamation of the prototypical social relation – father to
son – for Bloom and Stephen.

Thus fortified, Bloom enters Barney Kiernan's pub in episode
12. The bar is surcharged with latent violence: from one corner
the drunken Bob Doran appears ready to take offence at any
remark; at the center stands the "Citizen," a cartoon of the
most aggressive stupidities of Irish cultural and political
nationalism. Here Bloom should be on the run; the Citizen
wants to flush and hunt the fox of his (usually elusive) Jewishness. Bloom drops his normal reticence about confrontation,
however, and stands his ground: " – And I belong to a race
too, says Bloom, that is hated and persecuted. Also now. This
very moment. This very instant" (12.1467–1468). The familiar
correspondence between the two subject peoples, the Israelites
and the Irish, provides the obvious point of Bloom's analogy,
while the nearly contemporary boycotting of Jewish merchants
by the Irish in Limerick obstinately complicates that correspondence with Bloom's own sense of victimage. For the intensives
he scores into these final phrases surely catch the stress of
events most present and personal: Molly's tryst with Boylan
was delayed past 4:00 p.m., and Bloom might rightly sense it
happening *at this very moment*. Thus he repeats the themes
played musically through "Sirens," exhibiting a self-possession
attained with that awareness. He expatiates, angling the
language of grievance at Israel's fate to the actual point of
usurpation in his own home, the chains of domestic slavery in
"Calypso" shaking in the last phrases here: " – Robbed, says
he. Plundered. Insulted. Persecuted. Taking what belongs to

us by right. At this very moment, says he, putting up his fist, sold by auction in Morocco like slaves or cattle" (12.1470–1472). The language of racial dispossession conveys Bloom's sense of personal loss in code, like the music of "Sirens," but the awareness attained there leads to and legitimates his feeling of public indignation.

Is this righteous indignation expressed in the wrong language, however? After all, the dank den of Kiernan's pub teems with characters who vent their private anxieties and personal frustrations in words of retaliatory nationalism. To this unhappy fraternity Bloom seems to belong all too well; a fierce self-estrangement like theirs may be all that his new fortitude of self-possession comes down to. Does the private subject's going public entail merely an adoption of manias occasioned and sanctioned by historical oppressions? How Bloom counters this dire liability shows the full force and effect of Joyce's feminization of epic, which here opposes the Citizen as Cyclops, as gigantic cartoon of male consciousness, to Bloom's womanly Odysseus.

The Cyclops, his one eye bulging in the middle of his forehead as caricature of phallocentric single vision, promotes a politics of xenophobia, a patriotism premised on intolerance of the other. (The attitude is amplified in the stylistic parodies of this episode, which inflate one voice at a time to grotesque – if comic – proportions.) To this Bloom responds as heroine of the woman's sensibility described by Butler, who heard in the colloquial voice of the *Odyssey* a soft current of understatement, a gentle but constant irony that demonstrated, in effect, her capacity for double vision. Here Bloom's alternative vision is the larger and better view, the ideal country he proposes in response to the Citizen. It includes doubleness equally in the style of its articulation and the make-up of its citizenry, the two-gendered populace for which Bloom professes his concern:

– But it's no use, says he. Force, hatred, history, all that. That's not life for *men and women*, insult and hatred. And everybody knows that it's the *very opposite of that* that is really life.
– What? says Alf.
– Love, says Bloom. I mean the *opposite of hatred*. I must go now ...
(12.1481–1485; emphases added)

No less important than the message is the form of utterance: negating the contrary, Bloom shows his own *habitus*, his ingrained tendency to see the two sides of an issue. This phrasing also recalls a signature style in the archly male world of Old English heroic poetry − *litotes*, or understatement by negating the contrary − but, in the context of Bloom's character and the concern he professes here for men *and* women, that mannerism is also an intellectual marker. Its doubleness signals the first and necessary condition for the gender-inclusiveness Bloom sets against the male hypertrophy of the Cyclops. Here is a triumph of sensibility that presents Bloom's own version of the conquest won by heroines in nineteenth-century fiction: the victory of "female" temperament over the power and authority inherited through the male line is, through Bloom's speech, a marriage that is also a reconciliation of the two sexes − a setting of male and female, in this ideal state, against the Citizen's manic *patria*. If Joyce's fusion seems to represent an appropriation of the female by the male, Molly's voice will emerge in the final episode like the principle of resistance, an affirmation of the very otherness that makes the game of reconciliation worth its candle.

13−15
A mythic match

The two psychological subplots of Bloom's odyssey − his admission of the Boylan affair, his adoption of Stephen as son − crest and converge in episode 15, in the midnight realm of "Circe." The first of these subplots finds consummation as Bloom releases the needs and fears he has repressed during the day, now in the phantasmagoria of Nighttown. In this arena the long-avoided sight of Molly's union with Boylan is staged (15.3787−3819), and the undistractible eye of the dream holds Bloom to a scene that intimates the deeper truth of his own part in the affair. Complying with Boylan's directive to take up a keyhole view of the event, he rises to voyeuristic enjoyment, an excitement finely pointed in his exclamation: "(*his eyes wildly dilated, clasps himself*) Show! Hide! Show!" (15.3815).

The whole counterrhythm of showing and hiding that has marked Bloom's drama of recognition as avoidance conforms to the rhythms of a substitute desire, one which is both identified and satisfied in this final prospect. The therapeutic effect of Bloom's dream disclosures − he is perceptibly restored in the Nostos − may follow from a scene that characterizes and intensifies the strategy he has pursued from day into night, throughout his odyssey of recognition.

Bloom achieves this recognition in the dream sphere, but its fulfillment lies in the exteriorization of the private subject, in the restoration to the individual of a wholeness of social relation. This movement is reenacted summarily in "Circe," its significance restated and climactically expanded, as Bloom's inner agon leads immediately to an affirmation of his social potential, as we shall shortly see: to his assumption of the parental role toward Stephen. This bonding will be coded in the symbolism of dream, in a language that is at once hieratically private and charged with the historical and civil import of their relation. The connection is no less secretly nurtured, that is, than it is socially valued. This double measure captures the sense of balance intrinsic to the joint project of *Ulysses*, which recovers the private experience of novel characters in its most radical form and routes it back toward the public ground of epic. Joyce deepens this sense of equilibrium over the last third of the book. Even as Bloom and Stephen develop their acquaintance and so turn outward to history and society as the full ground of their relation, Joyce's stylistic exercises serve increasingly to set up interference fields between the reader's empathic response and the characters' inward experiences, which grow more private and mysterious as a result. (That Joyce's energies in episodes 13−14 and 16−17 run to stylistic elaboration makes the next chapter a better place for their sustained consideration.) This double rhythm returns a depth of elementary feeling to the social relation of father and son, which Joyce presents, in "Circe," with a complexity requisite to Stephen's struggle with the idea and facts of fatherhood.

Simon Dedalus appears to Stephen in a dream scenario. Natural father and son are cast here in the roles of Daedalus

and Icarus, a typology already associated with Stephen's failure
to soar as an artist:

Stephen
No, I flew. My foes beneath me. And ever shall be. World without
end. (*he cries*) *Pater!* Free!

Bloom
I say, look ...

Stephen
Break my spirit, will he? *O merde alors!* (*he cries, his vulture talons
sharpened*) *Holà!* Hillyho!

(*Simon Dedalus' voice hilloes in answer, somewhat sleepy but
ready.*)

Simon
That's all right. (*he swoops uncertainly through the air, wheeling,
uttering cries of heartening, on strong ponderous buzzard wings*)
Ho, boy! Are you going to win? Hoop! Pschatt! Stable with those
halfcastes. Wouldn't let them within the bawl of an ass. Head up! Keep
our flag flying! An eagle gules volant in a field argent displayed.
Ulster king at arms! Haihoop! (*he makes the beagle's call, giving
tongue*) Bulbul! Burblblburblbl! Hai, boy!   (15.3934−3950)

Stephen-Icarus's claim to fly coincides with a declaration of
independence from his father, who appears to disabuse the
boy of that illusion. "An eagle gules volant in a field argent
displayed" is the coat of arms of the Joyces of County Galway
(a red eagle in horizontal flight with its wings expanded −
"displayed" − on a silver background): these heraldic images
connect Stephen's ambition for flight to the family legacy, which
also provides the cries of falconry as the common language of
father and son. Thus Stephen's wish to escape Ireland on the
wings of his art merely lives out the will of the family and
country (and church) whose nets he had sought to fly by:
"keep *our* flag flying," the father cheers to the son's would-be
independence of flight. The whole enterprise Stephen myth-
ologized in *Portrait* is profoundly compromised, animated by
values of familial prominence − the very ethic he sought to
reject.

   This truth shows a depth of ironic cruelty that moves
naturally to disclosure in "Circe," in the oblique codes of the
dream. But the possibility of Stephen's escape from that bind

is also conveyed in symbolic language, in this exchange with Bloom:

Stephen
(*He fumbles again in his pocket and draws out a handful of coins. An object falls.*) That fell.

Bloom
(*stooping, picks up and hands a box of matches*) This.

Stephen
Lucifer. Thanks. (15.3593–3599)

Lucifer, Irish idiom for a match, is also the fallen angel — double and counterpart for the fallen Icarus. Picking that up, Bloom presents Stephen with a token that identifies him as the fallen angel of art. "Lucifer" utters Stephen's recognition in typological code, a premonition that seems to percolate until he attempts to deny that truth, some minutes later, when he asserts "*No, I flew*"; when the dream of his father will show him conclusively the folly of flight. What Bloom sets going in Stephen, then, is an intimation of both failure and the very unworthy effort of success, an awareness that will free the young artist from his self-defeating attempt to revolt (Lucifer-like) against Simon Dedalus and Ireland.

This alternative parentage promises a change in the artist's relation to history, too. Stephen's adversarial, escapist attitudes to history produced the fiction of Dedalian transcendence and the trope of the nightmare from which he was trying to awake (2.377). Thus, when Bloom wakes Stephen from a dream near the end of "Circe," he calls him (for the only time) by his first name (15.4928), discarding the surname that projected the whole myth of artistic transcendence. Further: Stephen recites his dream images on being awakened, and of these the most suggestive is the "black panther" (15.4930). This figure looks back to the image of the (black) leopard in which Stephen first apprehended Bloom, on the steps of the library at the end of episode 9, when the older man moving behind was sensed as the "step of a pard" (9.1214). Minus "Leo," this delionized beast repeats (and now perhaps redeems) the "Poldy" diminutive to which Molly reduced her husband; this gentler creature locates a value of peaceability that is brought to the first meaning of "black panther" now. A figure of primary terror in Haines's dream of the night before, it has already been turned into an emblem of England's colonies by Stephen, who dovetails references to Ireland and India in labeling Haines the "panthersahib" (3.277). The image of the black panther is indeed heavy with the nightmare of history, with the fury of imperial conquest, usurping possession, artistic exile; from it Stephen wakes to the new parent, Bloom, whose simple but intimate solicitude seems to be taken from his domestic center of value, from the feminine strain in his Odyssean role. Rather like Rochester, battered and remade at the end of *Jane Eyre*, Stephen enters a new order of female feeling that is domestic in source but, as in much women's fiction of the nineteenth century, implicitly or potentially political in effect.

Thus Stephen reopens his relation to history by recovering a parent – indeed both his parents (his initial concerns turned mainly around his mother) – in Bloom, who uncovers the full richness of a dually gendered role. These beneficial returns may represent the reclaiming of a collective legacy, Stephen's portion of an inheritance like that restored for Telemachus by Odysseus. Is this Joyce's version of the social restoration that attends the end of epic, where the reunion of father and son renews equilibrium in the external, political dimension of the palace? That Stephen's gift be conferred through the secret language of dream, from inferences drawn in a reading of psychic and mythic symbols, suggests the distance between the public and private spheres of epic and novel. Acknowledging this difference, his experience expresses a most earnest and urgent continuity of concern with the epic quest.

III
Nostos
16–18
The circle opened

The action of return in the last three episodes includes Bloom's movement with Stephen back to Eccles Street and the rejoining, in physical propinquity if not in sexual relation, of Bloom and Molly. The paternal and filial quality of the bond between the two men is clearly inferred, and so claims that portion of its likeness to Homeric epic, while the reunion of Odysseus and Penelope is achieved under the form of memory, in Molly's reminiscence of her first – primary – affections for Bloom. The special inflection Joyce strikes into the relation of Bloom and Stephen echoes Butler's emphasis on the female element in the *Odyssey*: the characters share cocoa across the kitchen table in episode 17 ("Ithaca"), and Joyce thereby raises the domestic circumstance to epic prominence, so framing the double-gendered identity of Bloom's adoptive parentage. If this synthetic character represents another mode of reconciliation in a book committed to concords, however, the domestic definition of the female may betray male authorship (subjection), and so turn the very solution it proposes into another form of the old problem of domination. Has the female been wholly appropriated by the end of *Ulysses*; is the concord promised at the end of the book merely a man's Pax Romana, its last word the "yes" of female subjection?

To this possibility Molly's monologue seems to say "no." She is unrepressed, certainly, when compared to Bloom's condition in the earlier chapters; she acts out verbally the energies shoved under, variously, by the romantic and domestic subjectivities of Stephen and Bloom. And as Vicki Mahaffey has argued, Molly's usage provides model and type for the stylistic exercises, the high verbal comedy, that courses through the second half of the book (analyzed in the next chapter here). The misrule of her inward monologue may be subvocal, but it is no servile subject's. She knows what men leave out – "a nice word for any priest to write and her a–e as if any fool wouldnt know what that meant I hate that pretending" (18.490–491) – and insists on living out such forbidden things, here textually: "I wanted to shout out all sorts of things fuck or shit or anything" (18.588–589). Resisting domestication and its several subjections, her independence makes for livelier, less conventional, more interesting reconciliations. Of these the most compelling lies in Joyce's rewriting of Homer, for his conversion of ancient epic into the terms of the modern novel is completed through the aegis of Molly. It is an achievement no less important than it is difficult.

In the *Odyssey*, where the hero's return to Ithaca closes the circle of his wandering, the axis of return is spatial; in *Ulysses*, as Molly turns back to an earlier time and recovers this moment as an instance of new possibilities for the future, the mode is temporal. These two modalities spell a more profound disparity of values: the old epic conceives its deeds under the limits of the actual and completes itself in the unwavering dimension of (pre-Einsteinian) space; the modern novel opens its characters' emotions into a zone of pure potentiality, which is wholly a function of time. This difference defines the main point of contention in *Time and Western Man*, where Wyndham Lewis, a man of the eye and a believer in fixities and definites like those engraved in Homeric space, pits himself against the art of the merely possible; against the timeful music of *Ulysses*. The two sides of this difference are also gendered by Lewis, who assigns the penetration and mastery of space to the male temperament, to the female the cultivation of sheer potentiality in time – the "what if?" world of words, the warm but wishful indecision of fluid chants like Gertrude Stein's.

Characteristically, Lewis has defined an opposition already reconciled by Joyce, especially on the last page of *Ulysses*. Here he leaves the signs of a battle waged between rival modes of consciousness, opposite apprehensions of space and time; he bridges the gender difference, as defined by Lewis, as the last of his massive syntheses. For Molly assimilates the image of the circle, with its male promises of spatial security and solidity, to the female idea of novel possibility, of endlessly renewable potential. (These symbolic values vary the more conventional ones, where the female is typically associated with the enclosing circle and the male with the linear and progressive, but Lewis's variation only confirms the arbitrary or plastic character of such an imaginative vocabulary.) To achieve her synthesis, however, Molly will need to purge that picture of cursive or linear movement of its more sinister implications – of forces, like vectors, at once compelling, coercive, betraying. And in doing so she extends into her own language a disquisition on history that Stephen originated.

"But O," Stephen exclaims to Bloom in the cabman's shelter, "oblige me by taking away that knife. I can't look at the point of it. It reminds me of Roman history" (16.815–816). Stephen's resistance to the knife-image here may indicate a process of temperamental change, one that has brought him out of the characterization hinted at in Buck's nickname for him, "Kinch, the knifeblade" (1.55). But the menace Stephen figures into the image of a knife-like continuum of time represents his long-nurtured response to the goal-oriented scheme of history that Mr. Deasy recited to him fifteen hours earlier. A sense of an ending like Deasy's preoccupies the imagination of *Ulysses* now, in the Nostos, as the narrative reaches toward its (expected) completion. Joyce puts time on the line, representing the vicissitudes of history conceived as linear progression (a spatialization of time that Bergson proposed as the root fallacy in western thought about temporality). Sequence in *Ulysses* is a model of betrayal: a deferral of meaning or reward to a later point in a series, Stephen knew as early as 10 a.m., is bound to be disappointed. And so the betrayals in *Ulysses* proceed under the sign of sequence, most notably in "Ithaca," where Bloom depicts the line of lovers filing (in his imagination) through Molly's bed and describes, with serio-comic eloquence, the deceptions that lie in wait, in series:

each one who enters imagines himself to be the first to enter whereas he is always the last term of a preceding series even if the first term of a succeeding one, each imagining himself to be first, last, only and alone whereas he is neither first nor last nor only nor alone in a series originating in and repeated to infinity. (17.2127–2131)

Joyce's case against the deceptions of linear time reaches into the printed fabric of Molly's monologue. As she lines up her lovers (beginning here with Bloom) in "Penelope," she spells and shapes the cardinal numbers in interestingly different ways:

I liked the way he made love then he knew the way to take a woman when he sent me the 8 big poppies because mine was the 8th then I wrote the night he kissed my heart at Dolphins barn I couldnt describe

it simply it makes you feel like nothing on earth but he never knew
how to embrace well like Gardner I hope hell come on Monday as he
said at the same time four I hate people who come at all hours
(18.328−333)

Since Molly presents nearly all her numbers in arabic figures,
the exception here (and below) is notable. She spells out "four,"
the hour of betrayal, which adds the motif of deceit or disappointment to this conspicuously linear formation of letters.
Another exception is also "four," which compounds the idea
of deceit yet again with the writing of letters in a line: "I could
write the answer in bed to let [Boylan] imagine me short just
a few words not those long crossed letters Atty Dillon used to
write to the fellow that was something in the *four* courts that
jilted her after out of the ladies *letterwriter* when I told her
to say a few simple words" (18.739−743; emphases added).
Like the promise of linear time, a string of letters on the page
unravels to betrayal. Against the constant prospect of the cheat
to which an end-deferring continuum must run, however,
stands the tonic possibility of the instant, already claimed and
whole, in the passage above; in the figure of "8," an integer
available all at once to the eye and, laid on its side, like the
recumbent Molly, a sign of infinity, of all time present and
fulfilled in the Now. Yet the very condition of print that
preserves Molly's monologue (or so the necessary fiction of publication goes) must dissipate the charge of its cosmic moment,
leaking it through the waste sad time of letters stretching before
and after. How, if at all, can Joyce hold Blake's infinity in a
grain of verbal sand?

"But O," Stephen exclaimed; his sound appears on the page
in an image that counters the picture of linear history that
follows. Occurring constantly throughout Molly's monologue,
"O" signals more than the wonder it expresses so persistently,
unsentimentally, splendidly. It punctures the militant continuum of print. A symbol shaped like the mouth that produces
it, "O" encloses a vocal moment on the page, drives a hole into
the time-woven fabric of written words, and projects a wholeness of feeling as a possibility known as closely as its speaking
present; as its own exclamation. It opens as it were into the

infinitely expandable instant of anecdote, the seamless and elastic moment of Molly's speech. An apparently fluid, open, improvisatory monologue finds center and stay, lexical and temporal constant, in that expression; "O" puts the tale in the mouth, enclosing a time-driven print in the no-time Joyce assigns to this episode in the schema.

Where epic turns its plot of circular return in space, then, Joyce's novel conspires to enclose time; to frame and release significant instants – Molly's, ultimately – from the dreary continuum of the quotidian. These high points are moments of grace, donations, gratuities that redeem the otherwise un-forgiving logic of linear time, those laws of necessary cause-and-effect that govern sequence (in a series that ever cheats on its promise and leads only to deceit). Consider the benefice conferred in this passage from "Ithaca," a chapter that features a (would-be) taxonomic precision of language, a no-nonsense objectivity in the questions it expects straight (correct, linear) answers to:

What spectacle confronted them when they, first the host, then the guest, emerged silently, doubly dark, from obscurity by a passage from the rere of the house into the penumbra of the garden?

The heaventree of stars hung with humid nightblue fruit.

(17.1036–1039)

The cosmic prospect sounding through the heavily voweled music of this response celebrates a rounded totality of existence, the very comprehensive significance that Lukács extols as the condition and gift of epic. And where the reunion of father and son centers this wholeness in Homer's epic, so the parental and filial relation of Bloom and Stephen recovers this high function here. If the epic inference is a gift, hardly a necessity, at most a suggestion, there is good reason to accept it. For the value of gratuity finds a testament at the very center of *Ulysses*, a review of which may conclude this chapter.

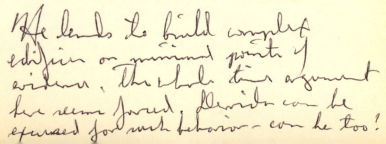

IV
"Wandering Rocks" and the art of gratuity

The rocks that wander in the tenth episode of *Ulysses* have been
given little freedom of movement, at least according to Joyce's
schema and the critical legacy it has fostered. "Mechanics,"
the declared art of the chapter, seems to allow no roving chance
to attend the progress of characters and events through its
nineteen sections. And his special technique of intrusion or
intercalation — inserting into one episode a detail from another,
which turns out, on examination, to be exactly simultaneous
with the point of entry — reinforces the sense of an overarching,
determining, master schedule. When the chapter is seen as a
microcosm of the novel, occurring at the midpoint and offering
its eighteen episodes (plus coda) as a miniature version of
Joyce's eighteen chapters, the standard of mechanical necessity
tends to be affirmed as a salient value of the book. There is
good reason to question this critical vision, however, for its
rule of orderly necessity begins to break down from this very
point in the novel. The gradually expanding stylistic exercises
in the second half delight increasingly in irrelevance, in various
non-functional elements — in the gratuitous enlargement of
style over the necessities of plot or action and the burgeoning of
details beyond any cause-and-effect sequence. Does the whirring
mechanism of "Wandering Rocks" whisper another value,
then, one that challenges the critical model of the well-tempered
time-piece; one that proclaims, at first subtly or tentatively,
the very principle of gratuity that is celebrated and indulged
increasingly from here on in *Ulysses*?

Long-established critical attitudes have made it difficult to
hear the grace notes in this episode. Scholars swayed by the
power of the schema tend to affirm the value of the mechanical
here. Stuart Gilbert grounds it in the brief Homeric description
of the Wandering Rocks (Odysseus avoided these to sail his
passage through Scylla and Charybdis); Gilbert suggests that
their clashing together at regular intervals — in striking contrast to Homer's usually anthropomorphic and non-mechanical
presentation of natural phenomena — provides a model

mechanism for Joyce's chapter. The same principle informs the well-documented account of Clive Hart, who carefully times and accurately synchronizes the primary narratives and their intruded details. Yet Hart takes this wheel of temporal control a turn further. He attempts to point out necessary thematic linkages, in his phrase "*causal relationships,*" between the narratives and the interruptions Some of the intrusions clearly support Hart's justifications: the cross-cut in section 1 from Fr. Conmee's walk to the promenade of "Mr Denis J Maginni, professor of dancing &c" (10.56ff.), points up the self-advertising, self-ingratiating aspect of their apparently disparate characters; the "Bang of the lastlap bell" (10.651) of the bicycle race is dubbed into the auctioneer's gong of section 11 to announce, fittingly and ominously, the "last lap" of the Dedalus household, now pawning Stephen's books. Signal instances like these, however, lead Hart to ignore his own cautionary admission — he concedes that reasons for some of the intrusions remain obscure — and to see the urban chronotope of "Wandering Rocks" under the total control of Joyce's schematic imagination, here animated by a scrupulous meanness indeed. "The mind of the city," Hart affirms, "is both mechanical and maliciously ironic." The emphasis on mechanism serves to limit the possibilities of characters — an oppression that weighs out its debt, however, to determining schemes like Hart's, like those that block critical attention to the value of imaginative generosity in Joyce's novel.

This alternative possibility needs to be opened. For Joyce does not retrieve the wholeness natural to epic (or fail to do so, according to a Lukácsian analysis) through the operation of schematic totalities like those exercised, variously, by Gilbert and Hart. The force that recovers epic fullness in *Ulysses* — first in the parent–son relation followed in this chapter, then in the linguistic attitudes and practices examined in the next — appears gratuitously, as the benefice of an energy larger than the designs of necessity, personal or otherwise. And defiance of the mechanical sounds most subtly but tellingly in "Wandering Rocks," where the interruptions run like fissures in the edifice of total control; where the intrusions break temporal progression, disrupt the linear sequence of narrative, fracture the necessary chain of cause and effect. Thematic critics may attempt to forge links between the intrusion and the new context, but most of these interruptions occur for no good reason — which is a good reason, the rationale and right of the gratuitous.

The gift is certainly a prevalent motif in "Wandering Rocks," as the exposition here will reveal, but Joyce's interests are not exclusively moral. If technique is the test of a man's sincerity, as Pound counseled, it is here a measure of a man's generosity. Joyce repeatedly links his intrusive method to the value of gratuity, complementing these interruptions with emphasis on the idea of the benefice. And so an inventory of gifts in his central chapter may be developed toward a concluding reassessment of its role in the novel and of the central values it frames.

The main narrative of section 2 occurs in the undertaker's shop in which Corny Kelleher works. The second of its two interruptions is taken from the next section, the story of the one-legged sailor's alms-begging progress up Eccles Street. The instant Joyce isolates for the intrusion in section 2 is the flinging of a gift — Molly's, as we learn later — to the beggar:

> Corny Kelleher sped a silent jet of hayjuice arching from his mouth while a generous white arm from a window in Eccles street flung forth a coin.   (10.221–223)

Merging the arc of the spat hayjuice with the trajectory of the coin, and using the conjunction to hinge the two images, Joyce presents two entirely disparate actions as single and continuous. Does this trick of the eye bind the two movements together by necessary cause and effect? The "causal relationship" posited here by Hart is the thematic opposition of Corny Kelleher's cult of death and Molly's affirmation of life, but only the first of these ideas has any presence in the episode, and it exerts no pressure. That interpretation seems to exercise a gratuity more properly located in the passage itself. For the narrative is interrupted in a way that is identified with Molly's gift and celebrated as such. It is the exemplary site for the beneficent intrusion.

And Joyce doubles its thematic valence as he plays the scene out fully in section 3, where the donation is twice given:

A plump bare generous arm shone, was seen, held forth from a white petticoatbodice and taut shiftstraps. A woman's hand flung forth a coin over the area railings. It fell on the path.

One of the urchins ran to it, picked it up and dropped it into the minstrel's cap, saying:

– There, sir.   (10.251–256)

The value of gratuity is pointed in relation to its opposite in section 5. Here the main narrative, telling of Boylan's purchase of Molly's present at Thornton's, is interrupted by a look at Bloom, hunched over a book-stall buying her *Sweets of Sin*. These two gifts stand as the wrong and right end of things. Bloom's gift partakes suggestively of the gratuitousness of the interruption that offers it to view, while Boylan's is no gratuity at all. It is wrapped in the dark necessity of his own mechanical character; it is impatient, importunate, urging, as coercive as his vocal presence in this exchange with the shop girl: " – Can you send them by tram? *Now*? ... Send it *at once*, will you?" (10.314, 322; emphases added).

A more complex and interestingly textured example occurs in the last of the three intrusions in section 4. Here the main narrative recounts the meal of the Dedalus sisters. Its meagerness leads Boody to unbless their father, that benefactor *manqué* – "Our father who art not in heaven" (10.291) – and it moves Joyce to break the chain of the quotidian, the dreary and necessary way of their world, with another interruption, another challenge to the law of sequence. The dinner scene thus opens onto a view of the "Elijah is coming" throwaway, making its way down the Liffey:

A skiff, a crumpled throwaway, Elijah is coming, rode lightly down the Liffey, under Loopline bridge, shooting the rapids where water chafed around the bridgepiers, sailing eastward past hulls and anchorchains, between the Customhouse old dock and George's quay.

(10.294–297)

Joyce complements the gratuity of this interruption and expands its significance with an allusion to the ultimate largesse, the gift-love of Christ's passion — the "Blood of the Lamb" (8.9) has been inscribed as the sign and value of the Elijah throwaway from its first appearance in "Lestrygonians." And Joyce's own articulate syntax fractures the linear sequence of normative prose to announce "Elijah is coming" — an annunciation that teems with possibilities of deliverance, beginning with its own liberation from the continuum of conventional sequence.

No less intricate and artful is Joyce's exposition of the gratuity theme in section 8. Its primary narrative, Lambert's tour through a crypt at St. Mary's Abbey, is twice interrupted, the second time by the event in the final moment of section 1: the sudden, flushed emergence of the young man and woman from behind the hedge. There the transgressors passed into the hard gaze of Fr. Conmee, who "blessed both gravely and turned a thin page of his breviary. *Sin: – Principes persecuti sunt me gratis: et a verbis tuis formidavit cor meum*" (10.203–205). Another perspective is set up in section 8, where the main narrative, identifying Lambert's guest by name, glances through new eyes at the woman in the intrusion:

— The reverend Hugh C. Love, Rathcoffey. Present address: Saint Michael's, Sallins. Nice young chap he is. He's writing a book about the Fitzgeralds he told me. He's well up in history, faith.
The young woman with slow care detached from her light skirt a clinging twig.   (10.437–441)

The lady is seen, not through the juridical view of Fr. Conmee, who exercises a pompous clemency at best, a forgiveness too haughty to be true, but from the vantage of Rev. Hugh C. Love, that is, *you see love*, and love is what you see. That nominal allusion redeems any culpability, gratuitously, yes, but no more so than Joyce warrants with the benefice of that interruption. (Once these values are secured, a similar gift turns the meaning of the English word *Sin*, as intoned over Conmee's breviary, back to its true sense: a letter rubric in the Hebrew psalter, a directive for song to begin, it announces a potential music of forgiveness and redemption as gratuitous as its interlingual pun.)

These varied examples demonstrate a value that may underlie the very position "Wandering Rocks" occupies in the novel.

At one time (in a letter of 24 October 1920 to Frank Budgen)
Joyce thought of entering a section after "Scylla and Charybdis" as a musical interlude, as "*l'entr'acte*," a "*nocturne*"
with "absolutely no relation to what precedes or follows"
(*Letters* I, 149). He never composed this intermission, but
the sense of redemption from linear time that it would afford
already attends the art of interruption, the formative conceit
of "Wandering Rocks," which stands in its place. Add to
this the fact that Joyce has made a whole chapter out of an
event scarcely mentioned in the *Odyssey*, as such providing a
gratuitous addition to the main mythic frame. These several
strategies conspire to raise generosity to the status of primary
value, one that holds together a narrative surface of rich and
varied benefice: the constant supplications and occasional
successes of the one-legged sailor; Fr. Conmee's walk to the
Artane orphanage to arrange for the admission of one of
Dignam's children; Martin Cunningham's good offices on
behalf of the Dignam family; and, finally, the destination of
the vice-regal cavalcade, the "Mirus bazaar in aid of funds
for Mercer's hospital" (10.1268–1269), which Joyce has
rescheduled from the 30th of May to the 16th of June.

If charity begins at home, in winsome and spontaneous acts
like Molly's flinging of the coin, it seems to end in regulated,
institutionalized forms: the crowning example of the benefice
is the staged spectacle of the Mirus bazaar, here sanctioned by
the English lord-lieutenant (the Earl of Dudley's attendance is
in fact invented by Joyce). Along the same lines, Joyce's method
of gratuitous intrusion seems to become the most predictable
and perfunctory of mechanisms by the second half of the
chapter (after section 9), when he no longer accompanies it
with the gift motif to give the technique a higher thematic
valence. Mere clockwork seems to account for this artifice by
the end, when its forms have lost the elastic vitality of Molly's
gift and hardened into images of the very temporal necessity it
first sprang into life to contest. This process points suggestively
to models of cultural time in contemporary historiography,
particularly Oswald Spengler's *Der Untergang des Abendlandes*
(1918 and 1922; translated as *The Decline of the West*), which

employed the organic model of the four seasons to prescribe
the direction and decline of classical and western civilizations:
the prime season of young Mediterranean culture, the sap years
of early *medium aevum*, wind down gradually but inevitably
into the technocratic imperia of Rome and the greater nation-
states of the twentieth century, like the one represented here by
Dudley. Historical determinism of this order is indeed invoked
as a containing frame for "Wandering Rocks," which allows
that virtù of imaginative generosity to ossify over the course
of the chapter; natural *élan* declines to a sheerly mechanical
force in the pattern of a Spengler-like cycle. Yet this end
may appear as the destiny of any serial progression – its fate
a function of the conditions of advancing narrative, which
limits possibilities according to the logic of processes under
way. Can Joyce release his principle of gratuity, then, from
the closing prison-house of narrative time?

To pose this question is to ask how the idea of the gift
impinges on the language of "Wandering Rocks" – and
beyond. For it is obvious that the art of verbal largesse in
Ulysses becomes increasingly conspicuous after "Wandering
Rocks," beginning with "Sirens." How does Joyce's medial
chapter posit an example for what comes later?

The language of "Wandering Rocks," as Karen Lawrence
helpfully notes, begins to document in earnest what does *not*
happen; begins to interest the reader in the possibilities ousted
by any particular linear movement or plot. Another way of
putting this observation: Joyce is finding words for the
*ir*relevant; words are now manifestly superfluous, heaped up
under the sign of gratuity that inspires the verbal textures of
"Sirens" and later chapters.

Those later practices find an advance signal in "Wandering
Rocks," moreover, in the image Joyce offers for the very
normative conventions of language he is defying. It is the file
of letters H.-E.-L.-Y-'S, the perambulating advertisement for
the stationery shop that once employed Bloom. Snaking through
Dublin, these letters depict the conditions and conventions
of print: linear, progressive, the end- or meaning-directed
sequence of written prose. The mechanical element in this

configuration is depicted most conspicuously in section 7, where Joyce mirrors the marching file of letters with two images of mechanical sequence: Tom Rochford's contraption for numbering turns at the Music Hall; Miss Dunne typing the letters and numbers of the date:

> The disk shot down the groove, wobbled a while, ceased and ogled them: six.
> Miss Dunne clicked on the keyboard:
> — 16 June 1904.
> Five tallwhitehatted sandwichmen between Monypeny's corner and the slab where Wolfe Tone's statue was not, eeled themselves turning H. E. L. Y'S and plodded back as they had come.
>
> (10.373–379)

A cartoon of linear language, these letters file into the text in defiance of the very principle they typify: they enter through an interruption, a break in the chain of sequence. Accordingly, Joyce plays his trick on the laws of linearity. For the goal to which these letters march is empty: the line of printed characters leads to the void.

Yet the interruption of sequence locates an alternative possibility, a positive opportunity. When "'S" breaks off from the chain earlier in *Ulysses*, for example, and lags disconsolately behind, we enter the space of comedy. It is a particularly Bergsonian comedy, where laughter erupts at the frustration of the mechanical. A similar opportunity opens in the middle of words, when Joyce disrupts the march of letters toward that phantasmal final meaning and handles them as notes to be played; when he fulfills the words as musical material; when he enlarges the sound gratuitously over the normative sense. "Dolores shedolores," Bloom muses in hearing a song in "Sirens," where words are handled as verbal plastic; as a medium replete with possibilities of deliverance, like those he murmurs in the next phrases: "At me. Luring. Ah, alluring" (11.734). These possibilities of feeling are released by a logic no more determined or controlling than the chance verbal associations of the speaker, but they have gained their urgency and legitimacy from the ethical aesthetic of gratuity in the preceding chapter.

These techniques characterize the major initiatives of "Sirens," and so it is interesting to note that Joyce waited until he had begun drafting that later chapter to enter most of the interruptions into the text of "Wandering Rocks" (these additions would continue to be made through the long process of composing, revising, and amplifying subsequent episodes). Of course, he needed to have "Wandering Rocks" complete before he could intercalate details between its various scenes. But the writing of "Sirens" began to put into manifest verbal practice the principle of gratuity that these interruptions signal and celebrate, and it is the waxing of that spirit in "Sirens" – and throughout the remaining episodes – that compels Joyce to multiply the grace notes in "Wandering Rocks."

This centrally placed episode reveals Joyce's schema as an essential convenience, a necessary means of organizing the minute particulars in the represented surface of life. Conversely, it indicates that this schematic mentality does not partake of the hubris that Lukács imputes to modern novels. These mechanical contraptions do not allow Joyce to simulate the extensive totality of significance that is the right and property of epic. For the schema, like the schedule in "Wandering Rocks," stops crucially short of being the whole story. Epic wholeness emerges in *Ulysses* locally, gratuitously, in a language wholly idiosyncratic and genuine to Joyce, in moments of feeling like Molly's "O." Satisfying and discharging a rage for order in the author, the schema releases the imagination of the reader, as in "Wandering Rocks," into an alternative dimension, a gratuitous space, one in which the verbal music of *Ulysses*, like Molly's "O," will offer its splendid benefice.

Chapter 3

Lapsarian languages

In "Drama and Life" (1900), first of those undergraduate
writings to intimate its author's mature intelligence, Joyce draws
a distinction that prefigures a central tension and problematic
in *Ulysses*:

Human society is the embodiment of changeless laws which the
whimsicalities and circumstances of men and women involve and
overwrap. The realm of literature is the realm of these accidental
manners and humours − a spacious realm; and the true literary artist
concerns himself mainly with them. Drama has to do with the underlying laws first, in all their nakedness and divine severity, and only
secondarily with the motley agents who bear them out.   (*CW*, 40)

The force of determinist fate that Joyce assigns equally to drama
and society may originate in Attic theater, at least in its reconstruction by anthropologists contemporary with him, like Jane
Ellen Harrison and other members of the Cambridge School,
who tied its performance to seasonal cycles and stressed its
connection to collective and timely rites of fertility. The same
matrix of social needs and mythic rituals provides a source for
the Homeric poems, or so this classical scholarship argued and,
in doing so, allowed the 17-year-old to discern those "changeless
laws" in the *Odyssey* as well. Is Joyce auguring the determining
force that the Homeric schema will exert on *Ulysses*? If so, the
extent or completeness of that correspondence is already an
issue, for the absolute control of such archetypes is even now
resisted, here by "literature," an art of letters that can be
aligned easily with the stylistic high jinks of *Ulysses*. There the
exaggeration of literary mannerisms also opens into a "spacious
realm," which comprises more than two-thirds of the novel's
words. These "whimsicalities" can be heard to utter an antic
rejoinder to "changeless laws"; to amplify an energy utterly
at odds with the sublimely fated return of the Homeric plot.

Words are indeed the agents of this play, and Joyce dresses them correctly — with a suitably interlingual resource — in "motley": *mots de la comédie humaine*. The verbal brio of *Ulysses* is promised a species of freedom, then, and this convention- or fate-dismaying energy will succeed not despite but because of its capriciousness.

Like the spume that plays upon Yeats's paradigms, however, the happy abandon of style in *Ulysses* may defy the gravity of the inevitable only briefly. Just as the "motley agents" of 1900 *"bear out"* those "underlying laws ... in all their nakedness and divine severity," so the verbal panache of *Ulysses* may sound an equally determined music. The apparent detachment of these stylistic exercises from the individual protagonists, from the ordaining minds of the subjects, imbues the performance with an energy more mechanical than organic. "The higher the slavery," as Shaftesbury sardonically aphorized, "the more exquisite the buffoonery": the elegant hurdy-gurdy of Joyce's later chapters may only travesty — *trans-vestere* "to cross dress" — the naked and severe necessities it might otherwise redress; may conform to a force as automatic, unforgiving and unrelieved as those "changeless laws." The verbal fabric of *Ulysses* is indeed wound to a tension between necessary fate and comic possibility, an opposition that spells out the rival claims of the objective and the personal, the mechanical and the spontaneous.

These opposite possibilities cluster around a consideration of language published fourteen years later under the sponsorship of Joyce's benefactor, Harriet Shaw Weaver, on the pages of a journal that would soon serialize *Portrait*: the *Egoist* (1914–1919), formerly the *New Freewoman* (1913). The subtitle attached to both — *An Individualist Review* — professed a continuity of concern here. The tenets of radical Individualism were being established and tested in view of recent theory on the linguistic construction of personality, which included a consideration of the relation between individuality and language that was both psychologically and politically informed. This pan-European discourse provides a primary context for Joyce's verbal experiments: part of his legacy from recent and

His probably the first JJ critic to take D own / Marsden seriously (or to read her)

contemporary intellectual history, it establishes a critical
language close to his own moment, one which returns the
linguistic art and imagination of *Ulysses* to the high stakes
drama it really enacts: its struggle, in words, between the rival
claims of social necessity and individual freedom.

This international colloquy was shaped centrally by the work
of Max Stirner, the translation of whose *Das Einzige und sein
Eigentum* (1845) as *The Ego and Its Own* (1906; reprinted
six times before 1922) spread the major issues into popular
intellectual culture and impacted forcefully on the founding
editor of the *New Freewoman*, Dora Marsden, who continued
as leading contributor to the *Egoist*. Marsden extended Stirner's
nominalist critique of language and government, arguing the
irremediable opposition between Word and individual.
Language substitutes generic abstractions for concrete specifics,
she maintains, and thereby enacts the same kind of anti-
individualist generalization that is the work of every government, participatory or authoritarian (of all political beliefs the
most repugnant to Marsden is democracy, which appears to
her as a function and fallacy of language itself; as the social
institution of Word as class-concept, as averager, as leveler).
The disempowering processes of government occur only and
always, she insists, through language; through a human
credulity that is tapped and manipulated most perniciously
through the ear. Once the auditor allows the material body
of the Word to make real the substantive Idea, she warns, the
illusion of abstract presence is created; here is the spuriously
magic concept, the machismo authority, social governance.

This complaint against social institutions and their verbal
constitution certainly spoke to Joyce's own youthful anarchism,
a position with which Marsden allies herself irresistibly, if warily
(absolute anarchism resists any *ism*, just as the truest dadaist is
the anti-dadaist). While this discourse maintained that language
exerts a force of mechanical determinism only, and so works
ever against the desire for individual freedom, Marsden also
posited an alternative possibility, a means of delivery from the
prison-house of words. This possibility needs to be considered
in view of its promise and realization, for it outlines the logic

Jameson?

and consequences of one likely response to the issues Joyce presaged in 1900 and engages throughout *Ulysses*.

To avoid the illusion of the verbal token, Marsden turns to the visual Image, a monad she invests with the several values she finds betrayed by words. Fresh, unacculturated, ungeneralized, the Image offers a necessarily non-verbal means of direct, ultra-subjective sensation. As such, it forms the basis of individual perception, valid action. "The human brain can work to fruitful purpose only when it is set to ply about images," she proposes; these pictures "have sprung into vivid form in the human consciousness" without the mediating form of words. Images thus present realities as sudden, immediate, and radically particular as their authoring subject, who "is at home only in that aura of images which is thrown off from the living 'I.' " This vital individual is renewed moment to moment through the life of the visual sense, through "the whole gallery of images which it can throw off for itself; the stream of life and all the images which glow in the stream." Images are indeed the forcing agent of libertarian revolt against generic verbal abstraction and its residue in history, in politics: the dead generalizations of social convention. "The directing lures in life then are Images," she calls to fellow (individual) travelers, for the immediate "feelings" that are instinct with these images "can magnetize the vital power, first to attention, then to action." The path from fresh visual perception to revolutionary political activity is thus as direct as the sensation conveyed by the Image, and the rhetoric and pride of Marsden's editorials intimate its utopian possibility constantly.

Her epistemology, however, was only a hermeneutic of sense perception, and it could be made to sustain any one of several political values. As easily as her (pseudo)science of perception might endorse anarchism, and so appeal to the anarchistic socialism of Joyce's own past, it could be turned to support authoritarian tyranny as well, for the extreme particularity of the Image validated the autonomy of the Self, a kind of supreme individual. Anti-statist and libertarian as this radical subjectivity might appear, it could also serve the purposes of the tyrannical, self-authorizing Ego. Awareness of this alternative sets out the full range of options and implications for Joyce's response to the problems Marsden has formulated so cogently. And this alternate valence is clearly assigned to it in early 1914, on the pages of the *Egoist*, in a review of recent visual art by Ezra Pound.

In "The New Sculpture," Pound rehearses the linguistic issues in terms identical with Marsden's. To the inferior work of words he prefers the incandescent sight of sculpture by Jacob Epstein or Henri Gaudier-Brzeska, whose "art is to be admired rather than [verbally] explained." Feeling "sick of the psycho-intellectual novel," he rejects a genre and medium in which wordy complexities beget wordy complexities — "the analytical method of pretending that all hateful things are interesting and worthy of being analysed and recorded." He turns from the chicanery of verbal chic to the absolute Image, the unmediated presence and stark clarity of sculptural forms. As Pound's artist struggles free of language, moreover, his intelligence sheds it as the very debility of democracy — the generalization of identity — that Marsden has found in it. "The artist has been at peace with his oppressors for long enough," he declares, then specifies: "He has dabbled in democracy and he is now done with that folly." Heroic self, Pound's artist will produce an equally particularized image, but he develops this individualist value in the direction of *le moi supérieur*, the single figure of the dictator. To endow this authority he now summons "the spirits of our ancestors," declaring that "it is by them that we have ruled and shall rule, and by their connivance that we shall mount again into our hierarchy. The aristocracy of entail and of title has decayed, the aristocracy of commerce is decaying, the aristocracy of the arts is ready again for its service."

These sentences were heard earlier to echo and counterpoint Joyce's own youthful formulation for the social potency of literature. There the authority of Pound's aristocratic artist was seen in contrast with Joyce's sense of the writer's complicity in a collective, implicitly socialist mission. This is a point of ramifying difference, one that defines Joyce's singularity increasingly as his literary generation matures. For Pound's extension of Marsden's premise defines a line of thinking central to the radical modernism of Lewis and himself, one that accounts equally for their cultivation of visual aesthetics and authoritarian politics. Joyce's differences reach to social attitudes as well as aesthetic practices, which allow him to create the speaking character of the democratic average, Leopold Bloom, and to show that the individual remains irrepressible, ungeneralizable, an equal partner in transactions with generic words. For Joyce remains *verbally* engaged with those linguistic issues on which Pound has forced his authoritarian – *visual* – answer.

This engagement includes a debilitation of the radical individual through the working of words, and the first section of this chapter will follow this process through Joyce's own experience of writing the novel and the crises of the verbal artist Stephen Dedalus, who serves at least in this respect as Joyce's counterpart. Instead of straining words to the principles of a visual linguistic like Pound's or Lewis's, however, Joyce engages in a process of reimagining the relation between Self and language. He renews his sense of individuality as a function of a new linguistic understanding, one which works out the reconciliation between private subject and social totality, as discussed in the preceding chapter, in terms special to his apprehension of language. Here Stephen's romantic subjectivity and its attendant sense of Word will alter and merge into the more generic individuality of Leopold Bloom, whose operative sense of words accommodates a speaking personality at once common and private, historically and culturally conditioned but also endowed with an individual, indeed idiosyncratic vocabulary. This development from Stephen to Bloom will be followed as a newly discovered line of unity and continuity in *Ulysses*, to be examined for its depth of linguistic intelligence in the middle section of this chapter. Bloom will then be seen to exercise this linguistic as a poetics of the common man in the third and final part. The starting point for this consideration is the remarkable and conspicuous phenomenon of Joyce's stylistic carnival in the second half of the novel. Those exercises, no less than the implementation of the Homeric scheme examined earlier, take direction and meaning from the inner life of the protagonists, here from the deliberations on language (variously recondite and unselfconscious) by Stephen and Bloom, whose experience with words will eventually center the consideration.

I
Stephen Zero

The Rosenbach manuscript of *Ulysses* shows a line penned heavily after "Scylla and Charybdis" and the inscription: "End of first part of *Ulysses*, New Year's Eve 1918." This division coincides with a major shift in aims and methods. The life of the novel gravitated from external drama to the internal vitality of its various styles. This change came more suddenly − immediately after the composition of "Wandering Rocks" − than the final text of the novel suggests. It is obscured by the final revisions, as A. Walton Litz has demonstrated, when Joyce recasts many of the earlier episodes in forms that match his later sense of the novel's design. Of the first nine chapters the most extensively modified is "Aeolus." Joyce overhauled it in 1921, as he was drafting "Ithaca" and "Penelope," and he altered it in ways that match the main initiatives of the later chapters, "Ithaca" in particular. There the question-and-answer format serves to break up the flow of the story into discrete aesthetic units; in "Aeolus" the insertion of newspaper headlines fractures narrative continuum and, within those framed and arrested moments, allows the style to dilate in a fashion that clearly anticipates the expansiveness of later chapters. But the newspaper format offers more than a convenient opportunity for this performance. Here the medium of the public Word both characterizes and facilitates the linguistic power being released. The common tongue offers its resources as the source of this apparently autonomous energy of language, a force noticeably detached from the control and − it seems − felt life of the two protagonists, whose inward monologues, so differently pitched, individuated the usages of the first six chapters.

Depersonalization appears indeed as the theme word of Joyce's stylistic odyssey: *DE-per-son-are* "NOT to sound through." If *persona* originally owned meanings bound up with the mask through which Roman actors spoke their parts — themselves — in the play, Joyce seems increasingly to silence — or drown out — the subject as origin of his stylized noise. This project begins noticeably as the second half of the novel starts up, in "Sirens." As Derek Attridge has shown, Siren talk is depicted repeatedly as originating in, not merely issuing from, the lips: "miss Douce's wet lips said, laughing in the sun" (11.72); "Her wet lips tittered" (11.76); "Lenehan's lips over the counter lisped" (11.328); "miss Douce's lips that all but hummed, not shut, the oceansong her lips had trilled" (11.377–378); etc. The usual instrument of utterance is now heard to generate the speech and, in doing so, to void the words of intention, of an ordaining or superior individual. That "Sirens" bewildered Harriet Shaw Weaver, Joyce's benefactor, and dismayed Ezra Pound, his advocate, might well have troubled his equanimity, but it could hardly have surprised him. For the musication of language hushed the articulate Ego, the radical individual championed variously by those two readers.

This principle discovers its fully complex implications in the next chapter but one, in the profound serio-comedy of "Nausicaa," where laughter at a mechanically mannered speech touches the corner of something far darker. A little farce of contemporary manners sounds through Gerty MacDowell's character-in-voice, which echoes the language of popular romance, as purveyed in commercial advertising and cheap fiction. It is manifestly clear, however, that the consumer is consumed, equally spiritually and materially, psychically and verbally. Gerty is a quotation, a linguistic onion that unpeels to a center no less disturbing for the laughter Joyce generates out of that empty space. Gallows humor, its music knells the death of the expressive Ego, the privately authorized voice, the romantic subject already overthrown in the epic quest followed through the preceding chapter. The critical questions must now be put more starkly: could Gerty be Stephen's true Penelope; is that cypher of the self the aim and end of the former individual hero?

The sense of linguistic autonomy in *Ulysses* does coincide with feelings of authorial anonymity. The waxing powers of style measure the waning force of the self, and Joyce spells out this bitter ratio in his letters, in a vocabulary no less intense than oblique. He announces his practice of consuming the styles he uses in successive episodes in a letter to Weaver of 20 July 1919. The "burnt up field" (*Letters* I, 129) that each chapter in this scorched-earth campaign leaves behind depicts a wastage that appears as a feeling of personal depletion. When he writes to Weaver again on 24 June 1921, he describes the "task I set myself technically in writing a book from eighteen different points of view and in [not quite] as many styles" and assigns this enterprise – oddly, given the apparent fullness of its verbal surfaces – to origins of personal emptiness. "Here now is an example of my emptiness," he confides to Weaver, but proceeds to indicate what a hectic emptiness it is: "My head is full of pebbles and rubbish and broken matches and lots of glass picked up 'most everywhere'" (*Letters* I, 167). That first image of self-decimation provides a basis in the second for a portrait of the stylizing artist as gravitational vacuum, sucking in the *disjecta membra* of popular culture, or as *tabula rasa*, a blank slate that takes the imprint of discourses that originate outside him; that exist in his work as a function of his very absence as articulate individual.

Hyperactive styles may serve, conversely, as compensation for the loss of authorial power; the voiding of the self may be avoided, the silence filled with the burgeoning noise of those mannered parodies. This exchange seems to generate the verbal play of "Nausicaa," at least as Joyce describes the circumstances and motives of its composition in late 1919 and early 1920. "For six weeks after my arrival" back in Trieste, he writes to Frank Budgen on 3 January 1920, "I neither read nor wrote nor spoke" (*Letters* I, 134). Personal inertia and silence appear indeed as the condition and instigation for writing – "but as it cannot go on so I started *Nausikaa*" (*Letters* I, 134) – and in fact for writing that chapter in its extravagantly mannered fashion, in the "namby-pamby jammy marmalady drawersy (alto là!) style" (*Letters* I, 135) that he characterizes in the same letter. This enterprise is stimulated by anxieties of self-annihilation, and the progress report on *Ulysses* in the same letter speaks fears of emptiness, termination, silence: "So I started *Nausikaa* and have written *less than half ... Nausikaa* will be finished I hope. To *abandon* the book now would be madness" (*Letters* I, 134; emphases added). The novel's glass is half-empty, not half-full. Dread of the void may find some relief in stylistic high jinks, but the personal dispossession that this play is designed to disguise can only be deepened by this practice of writing away from the self.

The fate of the individual author, his demise linked to the autonomous powers of language, is lived out by Stephen. Archetype of the romantic subject, solitary high flyer of the Daedalus myth, he falls from prominence most visibly in those early chapters that show (through revisions and additions entered later in the process of composition) the first insurgency of an independent linguistic energy. In "Scylla and Charybdis," his lecture on Shakespeare is a monument to the myths of heroic privacy that inform his earlier conception of himself; from the smithy of Shakespeare's personal history and domestic life Stephen has "forged" a story of the making of great art. The person most significantly *un*convinced by that lecture is Stephen himself, who early on foretells his fall from intellectual prominence with an allusion to the sounds of Daedalus's counterpart, Milton's Lucifer, on the floor of hell: "*Ed egli avea del cul fatto trombetta*" (9.34): "and of his arse he made a trumpet." What Stephen's failure makes possible, among other things, is his participation in a supra-individual discourse: an antic and humane mockery of his own words. Thus Joyce unravels the former accord between the individual's inward monologue and a narrative that received him easily into its verbal weave; the language around Stephen is now an anti-Narcissus, an echo that turns the would-be sonorities of his cogitations into notes for musical follies:

– Bosh! Stephen said rudely. A man of genius makes no mistakes. His errors are volitional and are the portals of discovery.

> Portals of discovery opened to let in the quaker librarian, soft-creakfooted, bald, eared and assiduous. (9.228–231)

> The quaker librarian, quaking, tiptoed in, quake, his mask, quake, with haste, quake, quack. (9.887–888)

The sportive mood is purely verbal, its incipient hilarity a function of energies wholly and independently linguistic. The fun proceeds in Stephen's idiom, however, often in his own voice, and so shows the formerly private individual open and responsive to energies in language that lie outside his control.

The drama staged in "Scylla and Charybdis" has been rehearsed in the newspaper offices of "Aeolus." Here Joyce shifts the energy of words from the failing grasp of the private artist to the public domain. This exchange is recorded most subtly and searchingly in the fate of Stephen's story, "The Parable of the Plums," a *petit tour-de-force* that looks back through Joyce's early career for its import in *Ulysses*.

In it two old ladies set out on a day trip to Nelson's Pillar; their panting climb leaves them sitting quietly below, eating plums and spitting out the stones. Pathos tinged with quiet irony, this finale typifies the epiphanies that conclude the stories in *Dubliners* – "Dubliners" (7.922), Stephen murmurs just before he begins to recite the story, thus citing the collection in which it could have fit. This piece recalls most notably the ones composed during or before the moment of *Ulysses*: in June 1904 Joyce would be starting to write pieces for the childhood phase of the collection's chronological scheme ("The Sisters," first of these, was published in August 1904); the two ladies are indeed seen as affectionate aunts, as though from a boy's perspective, as in "The Sisters" or "Araby." Most important, those early stories recorded the resistance of the youthful character-in-voice, prime type of the individual artist, to the speech and mores of popular culture. Joyce's backward allusion in "Aeolus" checks the very motive and aim of such resistance. For Stephen's story is welcomed here by the newspaper editor Myles Crawford, agent and emblem of words in the marketplace. The irony reaches to the detail of Crawford's acceptance: his sole condition – he will print the story as long as the ladies "do no worse" (7.1031) – looks

back knowingly on those benighted standards of public morality
that Joyce himself campaigned against as individual artist, in
his near-decade-long battle to have *Dubliners* published.
Thus Joyce brings his old Dedalus to newly friendly ground in
popular culture. He rewrites the exquisitely crafted finale of
the "Parable," at the end of the chapter, in the comically
inflated style of a newspaper headline:

DIMINISHED DIGITS PROVE TOO TITILLATING FOR
FRISKY FRUMPS. ANNE WIMBLES, FLO WANGLES – YET
CAN YOU BLAME THEM?   (7.1069–1071)

Respelling the epiphany of the private artist in the words of a
common tongue gone amuck, Joyce takes verbal control most
conspicuously away from the individual, suggesting that the
energies of *lingua publica* are independent, irrepressible.

Where the romantic individual gives way to the public
discourse as the generative center of verbal art, Stephen hands
the mantle of artist to the Everyman character Bloom. What
rights and powers may be conveyed through this transfer is a
critical question to be addressed at length in the next section,
but it is necessary first to record the formal exchange. Following
the strategy just examined in "Aeolus," it occurs in "Nausicaa"
through an extended allusion to earlier work.

Bloom's appearance near the strand in "Nausicaa" and his
voyeuristic regard on Gerty recall Stephen's idealizing gaze on
the female figure on the beach near the end of *Portrait*. The
correspondence runs nearly point for point, as Fritz Senn has
shown. Stephen's bird-girl shows "delicate" (*P*, 171) legs,
and Gerty wishes above all to project "delicacy" (13.98, 120,
360); the ivory of the bird-girl's thighs reappears as the hue
of "ivorylike purity" (13.88) that Gerty attempts to achieve
cosmetically; Stephen's eyes "worship" (*P*, 171) just as Bloom's
"dark eyes ... [are] literally worshipping at her shrine" (13.563–
564). The word Stephen uses to describe the provocative fixing
of the seaweed on the girl's statuesque flesh – "fashioned"
(*P*, 171) – repeats to the manifestly different sense of the
epithet that governs Gerty's consciousness: Dame Fashion. If
Stephen's vision of the girl provided the moment at which he

resolved to be an artist, his aesthetic adheres to a standard of
classical purity that is preserved, in 1902, as an exception to
the norm; as the privilege of sequestered tastes; as the signature
of an elite individual. Bloom's prospect on Gerty is wholly
unindividuated − beginning with the fact that it is conveyed
from Gerty's own perspective, although that is hardly private
property, for her voice is saturated with the idioms and images
of the popular culture that "fashions" her.

Differences in the two episodes define the main lines of
development between the two novels, but Stephen's sense of
self in *Portrait* is a residual value at least sufficiently strong
to generate this echoing riposte in *Ulysses*. Can the language
of generic man and woman be reconciled with the values of
individuality? If Bloom's speech achieves such a synthesis, it
resolves the central problematic in Marsden's (and Pound's)
socio-linguistic, healing the breach that opens the main discursive space of the *New Freewoman* and the *Egoist*. But how
would individuality be reconceived to sustain such a reconciliation? The answer lies in an understanding of the linguistic
philosophy that *Ulysses* can be heard to articulate, and this
sense of language requires a sustained consideration.

II
Word incarnate, word carnival

Critical commentary over the last two decades has tended
increasingly to see Bloom as hero of *Ulysses*, to favor him over
Stephen as center of value in the novel. "There's a touch of
the artist about old Bloom," Lenehan remarks to M'Coy
(10.582−583), and recent criticism extends this affirmation,
taking Bloom-speech as type and exemplar of artistic language.
A growing emphasis on the importance of popular culture in
Joyce's conditioning and make-up has reinforced this critical
development. And so a commentator attempting to formulate
the philosophy of language in *Ulysses* can be led into a
dichotomy like the following. Bloom's ideolect provides a usage
as expansive and comprehensive (and inexact) as his Everyman
character; this sense of word stands manifestly at odds with

that of the neo-Scholastic Stephen, who is a lover (successful or not) of linguistic precision; whose words seek a meaning as integral and well-defined as the individual he fables in the myth of the solitary, transcendent artist Daedalus. Must this dualism be uncompromising? Yes, the heroic focus of the novel shifts, the usage loosens accordingly, but this development is accompanied by a series of linked passages, *topoi* really, which articulate an ongoing inquiry into language, a continuing revision in the text of its operative sense of word and an adjustment to its speaking character. If differences in the verbal temperaments of the two protagonists are meant to be bridged, the terms of engagement and reconciliation appear in these passages. They contribute an understanding of language as rich and strange as Stephen's hermeticism, but move toward attitudes of linguistic possibility as generous and inclusive as Bloom's. Here Stephen's hieratic subjectivity is reconceived as a function of the way language works, and this new sense of self, attuned to the usages of the verbal Everyman, reveals a continuity in the novel, a developmental unity wrongly lost by emphasis on differences between Stephen and Bloom.

The declared art of "Proteus" is *philology*, and Stephen's love of language extends through his verbal pyrotechnics into a semi-discursive recitation of linguistic philosophies. He opens the scene − his eyes − and reveals a strongly visual proclivity in his sense of the working of words:

> Ineluctable modality of the visible: at least that if no more, thought through my eyes. Signatures of all things I am here to read, seaspawn and seawrack, the nearing tide, that rusty boot.   (3.1−3)

Stephen obviously frames nature through language; he textualizes the plane of visual perception, *reading* natural phenomena as "*signatures.*" The critical question here goes to the claim such "signatures" make on "things"; to the relation between words and referents. Modern linguistic phenomenology regards language as mere appearance, no more the referent itself than the image (or phenomenon) under which the object is perceived. Yet Stephen seems to press these contemporary tenets back toward Adamic or Edenic myths of language. These legends posit an original usage in which words are inseparable from, indeed identical with, their visible meanings: "all things" find their proper "signatures" (this term suggests authenticity in the verbal identification). If such isomorphism seems hardly tenable as a linguistic condition in a post-Enlightenment era, it nonetheless expresses a hubris in the intellectual culture contemporary with Joyce, the one boasted on the pages of the *New Freewoman* and the *Egoist*, where Pound sought a similarly visual immediacy for words. And the sense of overweening authority that attended Pound's attempt to forge verbal images, to hold words close to the curve of things, appears here as a condition of Stephen's own verbal sensibility: "*ineluctable* modality of the *visible*."

What is there in Stephen's experience that might allow him to engage that linguistic vision more searchingly; to counter its delusive powers? In "Nestor" he has paused over the childish script of his pupil Cyril Sargent. "*Sums*" (2.128), the heading of the arithmetic lesson, is also (minus the final *s*) the first person singular of the Latin verb *to be*: "I am." Writing himself down, Sargent seems to have inscribed the creative Word. To that promise of absolute identity between word and essence, an appealing illusion, Stephen responds with appropriate complexity: "Across the page the symbols moved in grave morrice, in the mummery of their letters, wearing quaint caps of squares and cubes. Give hands, traverse, bow to partner: so: imps of fancy of the Moors" (2.155–157). That these symbols are numbers rather than letters adds to the sense of exact equivalence between sign and referent, and this is a possibility Joyce's verbal art serves to reinforce. The first clause here moves through three equal phrases, each paced to two iambic feet; the whole resolves into a feeling of intense musical concord, a strong rhythmical equivalent for the value of verbal correspondence. Yet Joyce turns the impression of absolute language on an obsolete word, "mor*rice*." Archaicism befits the Edenic element in the myth, but to achieve that sense of musical concord one must ignore the stubborn sound of the modern word – the trochaic "*mor*-ris." The dissonance is subtle, but articulate: the difference between the original and contemporary pronunciations sounds out the absolute distance between Eden and Ireland, the myth of first words and the world in which words actually work. And where Joyce softly heckles the myth of verbal mimesis, Stephen amplifies that challenge as he casts the whole idea of imitation in words as "mummery," a clowning or roguish take-off. The high rites of verbal mimesis dance only a sham likeness; the Adamic word, that antique dream, is going antic.

The vital skepticism of "Nestor" continues in "Proteus," persisting through the complex tonalities of its overture and extending into an alternate model of language. Here Stephen sees "the gunwale of a boat, sunk in sand. *Un coche ensablé* Louis Veuillot called Gautier's prose. These heavy sands are language tide and wind have silted here" (3.286–289). Not an array of incandescent signs, the language of nature is depicted here as sand. The image suggests heaviness, accumulation, a quasi-alluvial deposit from the past – a piling of meaning upon meaning in the variegated strata of each word. A telling shift has occurred in Stephen's attitude: the *natural* state of the langue is now *historical*. Over time words alter their meanings, and if such changes defy the stop-time claims of an original Edenic Word, they also constitute a vertical richness, a heaped and buried treasure of multiple significance. Stephen now seeks to lay hands on this hoard but only, it is crucial to note, by contributing to it: "Hide gold there. Try it. You have some. Sands and stones. Heavy of the past" (3.290–291). The verbal gold Stephen will hide in these deposits is a mineral enriched by the same tradition to which he is returning it. Words are indeed a self-accruing richness, and Stephen's contribution concedes his status as auxiliary, his role as instrument, in that temporal-historical process of linguistic enrichment. The individual who was formerly a source and governor of verbal meaning is now but a catalyst in a process whose energies use him.

The same principles are dramatized in episode 14, "Oxen of the Sun," most notably in the comprehensive sequence of the chapter: a seriatim progression of the ages of English prose, the history of styles proceeds as though autonomously, free of the ordaining control of any individual artistic sensibility. The whole language, as represented in this apparently self-generating and self-sustaining history, serves as origin and determinant of individual usage. This axiom is demonstrated most tellingly as Joyce allows the mannered styles to repeat words or phrases that once appeared to be Stephen's coinages: where his verbal flourishes rang as the fresh inventions of an individual word-smith, they are now heard as echoes or, at best, variations on patterns prescribed earlier in literary and linguistic history. For example, the exquisite anguish in Stephen's conjuring of his mother's shade — "a ghostwoman with ashes on her breath" (3.46−47) − repeats the maternity tropes, condenses the more expansive grandiloquence, of Milton's (or Hooker's) Latinate meditations, as imitated here by Joyce:

But thou hast suckled me with a bitter milk: my moon and my sun thou hast quenched for ever. And thou hast left me alone for ever in the dark ways of my bitterness: and with a kiss of ashes hast thou kissed my mouth.   (14.377−380)

While "Oxen of the Sun" presents the conception and gestation of the English language as its imaginative conceit, it portrays the unmaking of the archly individualist artist. To this point Joyce echoes and alters the words of the Apostles' Creed to stress, not the integral divinity of the phrase-making artist, but the biological individual's role as mere auxiliary or catalyst in the ongoing history of the language: "In woman's womb word is made flesh but in the spirit of the maker all flesh that passes becomes the word that shall not pass away" (14.292−294).

Stephen realizes these values with increasing force and self-consciousness, beginning in the Telemachia and extending into "Aeolus" and "Scylla and Charybdis." By "Proteus" he has loosened his hold on language sufficiently to participate in its energies as common resource. This power is found in his protean figures for the dog's movement across the strand (remarked upon in the previous chapter) and is extended in this next passage. Here his usage exceeds the monodic manner of his earlier isolation; he now tolerates otherness, holding these noticeably variegated strands easily, elastically, in one expansive weave:

> Morose delectation Aquinas tunbelly calls this, *frate porcospino.* Unfallen Adam rode and not rutted. Call away let him: *thy quarrons dainty is.* Language no whit worse than his. Monkwords, marybeads jabber on their girdles: roguewords, tough nuggets patter in their pockets. (3.385–388)

In this piece of heteroglossia, the "roguewords" Joyce casts into the magic blazon of italics are "no whit worse than" Adam's speech or its extensions in the verbal precisions of the Scholastic realist Thomas Aquinas. Thus the demotic brio of street lingo and bawdy song infuses the supposedly holy usage of "monkwords, marybeads," and that stream of sheer "patter" hardens its "jabber," accordingly, into "nuggets" of highest worth. This is an alchemical poetic, but one that works against its first convention, for Joyce eschews the values of hierarchy in the echelon of minerals. He allows the supposedly base material of common speech to enter into relation with other verbal elements and thus activates, in diversity, the full richness of linguistic matter.

"Oxen of the Sun" once again repeats and expands the realizations Stephen has achieved in his Protean discourse. Here the history of the language proceeds from the quasi-sacral precincts of its Anglo-Saxon origins (14.60–106): the dominant monosyllable of the Old English tongue reinforces a sense of connection between integral word and single thing, but this Edenic speech shifts by the end to the street lingo that accompanies the medical students' recess to Burke's pub (14.1440). More specifically, as Joyce concludes his imitation of Milton's Latinate style, he allows the word "Eden" to acquire a suffix from contemporary slang and so locates, in that one compound, the origin and end of language in this mythic history. Academic speech finishes into the demotic present, a destination to which Joyce arrives in comically regulated riot:

> And as no man knows the ubicity of his tumulus nor to what processes we shall thereby be ushered nor whether to Tophet or to Edenville in the like way is all hidden when we would backward see from what region of remoteness the whatness of our whoness hath fetched his whenceness. (14.396–400)

The surfeit of relative pronouns in this last clause continues the assault on the myth of the Edenic Word, turning the grammatical action of precise relation between word and referent − who, what, whence − into this antic chant.

Once Stephen frees his speech in "Proteus" from the Edenic Word and its semantic constraint, his grammar and vocabulary loosen so remarkably that he has perplexed critics, such as C.H. Peake, who have failed to notice the underlying and accompanying change in linguistic philosophy. And the new sense of word turns around a new sense of self. Whereas the romantic subject Dedalus imposed himself on language, seeking a meaning as single and integral as the individual in his mythic fiction, the new man Stephen exists in complicity with language as autonomous force, as resource of historically rifted meanings and socially differentiated usages. No longer a heroic solitary, pitting himself and his restricted meanings and narrowly drawn mannerisms against the energies of language, he is the center of a Bakhtinian dialogic; he is a node, a knot of linguistic energies charged by traditions equally literary and popular − a vortex-point through which the forces of the whole language come rushing. Already in "Proteus" the lyric "I" of passages like the following diffuses across varied lexicons, mixing a Parnassian ideolect with rogue's cant, syncopating the stately cadences of these first phrases with bumping, jargonish rhythms − a mixture concocted not for its own sake but to trap, exactly, the complex of "high" and "low" feelings he experiences at the prospect of the woman:

When night hides her body's flaws calling under her brown shawl from an archway where dogs have mired. Her fancyman is treating two Royal Dublins in O'Loughlin's of Blackpitts. Buss her, wap in rogues' rum lingo, for, O, my dimber wapping dell! A shefiend's whiteness under her rancid rags.   (3.375−379)

The rhetorical fiction of this passage dissolves any sense of the single individual as its speaking presence, yet its variety and particularity are keyed precisely to Stephen's − no one else's − modulating complex of sentiments. He realizes a fullness of emotional and intellectual life, that is, once he has passed through the boundaries of mythic individualism, which constrained equally his sense of artistic self and his use of language.

The reconstruction of Stephen's verbal personality as an overlay of socially and historically received words and usages records a change from Adamic myths to a conventionalist description of language. This process continues in Joyce's development of speaking character for Bloom, who enters in the next chapter, and whose usage bears the heavy impress of contemporary convention. The underlying continuity between Stephen's new attitudes to language and Bloom's own (largely unselfconscious) verbal values is signaled in a passage Joyce has designed to show Bloom echoing Stephen's earlier cogitations, extending and merging their premises into a poetics of the individual common man.

Bloom's walk on the strand in "Nausicaa" picks up where Stephen left off in "Proteus." Indeed, he picks up the same stick Stephen threw at the dog there and uses it to continue rewriting the essentialist myth of language:

Mr Bloom with his stick gently vexed the thick sand at his foot. Write a message for her. Might remain. What?
I.
Some flatfoot tramp on it in the morning. Useless. Washed away. Tide comes here. Saw a pool near her foot. Bend, see my face there, dark mirror, breathe on it, stirs. All these rocks with lines and scars and letters. O, those transparent! Besides they don't know. What is the meaning of that other world. I called you naughty boy because I do not like.
AM. A.
No room. Let it go.
Mr Bloom effaced the letters with his slow boot.   (13.1256–1266)

Bloom's fantasy of breathing on the pool recalls God's spirit moving upon the waters in Genesis, the Word incarnating the World, and so summons the prime type of essentialist usage. Against such aspirations, however, Bloom pens an identifiably fragmentary script; its divergence from the first, perfect, Word-created World is signaled here as he repeats the spelling mistake in Martha Clifford's letter – "I called you naughty boy because I do not like that other world. Please tell me what is the real meaning of that word?" (5.244–247). No Edenic field, this is the labyrinth of modern (Saussurian) linguistics, where a word finds meaning, not as it reproduces the essence of its referent, but by virtue of its difference from other words in the lexical or phonetic system – "word" is not "wor(l)d." (This matrix of near-misses is Bloom's natural environment, verbal ground for his propensity to get things *slightly* wrong.) Acquiring significance by difference and proximity, language is a shifting system of signifiers, of tokens that relate first to one another, not to their putative referents; the meaning defined by difference is assigned wholly and arbitrarily by convention. Yet that very disparity between word and world opens a creative space. "I ... AM A ...": I love (amo), I am Alpha (and Omega) ... the series of possibilities is richly indeterminate, its potential a function of the professedly incomplete fit between those fractured letters and whatever intention may have compelled him to write.

Given the difference between the haphazard fragments of Bloom-speech and the severe if unrealizable totality of the divine Word, why should Joyce allow Bloom to court the highest ideal of Edenic language? Pausing over his own prospect of natural language, over "*rocks* with *lines* and scars and *letters*," after all, he has echoed (translated) Stephen's Aristotelian affirmation of natural transparency in language, "limits of the diaphane" (3.4), as he explains "O, those transparent!". The magic letter of Molly's exclamation opens its rounded window here, but its promise of linguistic directness seems to extend into the void: once words are unstuck from things, directness of expression seems the chanciest of hits.

"He flung his wooden pen away. The stick fell in silted sand, stuck. Now if you were trying to do that for a week on end you couldn't. Chance" (13.1270–1271). The very autonomy of language – those resources of historically accrued meanings and socially determined usages outside the speaker's control – renders an individual subject like (the old) Stephen a compliant partner at most, one who might "score" his exact feelings mainly or only by luck. But if that partner were Everyman, an (admittedly) ideal personification of the common history and society lying behind the common tongue, its apparently autonomous powers are in fact inseparable from him. Shaped by those forces, he is their ineluctable monologuist, tapping the independent energies of language with a will as forceful as the pressures of the past, as deep as a collective speech. By relinquishing the more strenuous exertions of individual intent, the higher claims of conscious control, Joyce leads Stephen to the character-in-voice of Everyman, whose language will proceed by an automatic energy to its true and proper marks; in this sense all his accidents in speech, like the lucky hit of his "wooden pen," are essential.

How Joyce turns these precepts into the practice of Bloom-speech, allowing the essential accidents of words to happen within the protagonist's identifiably private frame of reference, provides the interest in the final section of this chapter. It is worth noting first, however, how self-consciously Joyce records the transfer of verbal power in *Ulysses*: from absolute verbal substantive to sheer linguistic accidence, from old to new covenants of the word. He celebrates this shift with an appropriately severe *hilaritas* in "Ithaca." Here Bloom recalls the signal instance of verbal accident scoring a direct hit, an event in "Lotus-eaters," where the chance remark he passes on to Bantam Lyons with his newspaper − "I was going to throw it away" (5.537) − is taken by Lyons as a tip to wager on Throwaway, who would win the Ascot Derby that day; the throwaway phrase goes straight to the target. The Ithacan narrator now rectifies and venerates such accidents, seeing the tip given to Lyons as the divine Word revealed to Moses, likening the paper tossed away to the tablets engraved with God's commandments, as Bloom appears "with the light of inspiration shining in his countenance and bearing in his arms the secret of the race [Hebrew, the Ascot], graven in the language of prediction" (17.339−341).

Stephen has reconceived the verbal subject as a gathering of linguistic energies, then, as the transmitter of those historical and social forces that have shaped the language. Bloom, manifestly the product of those forces and their language, will articulate a sense of self compatible with those larger powers.

The precept Stephen has learned so arduously, however, remains for the most part external to his felt life (not for lack of intensity but for shortage of time he has to demonstrate it). Bloom owns its values, I have suggested, as the birthright of Everyman, and he gives Stephen's achieved idea an easy practice, a natural voice, an internality at once deeply psychological and compatible with his own generic identity. In the mistake, the error that turns on the absence of individual intention and conscious control, lies his most expressive vocabulary, as we are about to learn.

III
Graphic lies

"A man of genius makes no mistakes. His errors are volitional and are the portals of discovery" (9.228–229). In the guise of Shakespearian analysis, Stephen is describing the dynamics of the Freudian slip – an intellectual debt suggested in the same chapter with mention of "the new Viennese school" (9.780). While Freud maintained that primary desires and fears are relegated to the unconscious, and so find release only in dreams or in "mistakes" that escape the conscious censor, Stephen's and Bloom's linguistic deliberations conspire to suggest that words afford a constant opportunity for the Freudian slip. Following the arc of Bloom's "wooden pen," a speaker finds the verbal mark of his feeling by relaxing the conscious monitor, thus allowing the secret to rise and find its word. While a Freudian linguistic may concede the faultiness of verbal intention, it offers another kind of efficaciousness for words, and Joyce adapts this potential with cunning brilliance in the interior monologues. Here Bloom raises the verbal specter of Blazes Boylan without ever citing him directly: a series of look- or sound-alike formations of the hated name summons Boylan, and these rhyming words serve equally to release Bloom's anxiety about his rival and avoid a head-on collision with that bounder. Distracting oneself from the horror, in other words, provides the only way of accessing and articulating it. This verbal practice may comport with the "female" temperament of Butler's *Authoress*, to whom he assigns "a kind of art for art's sake love of a small lie, and a determination to have things both ways ... She loves flimsy disguises and mystifications ... that mystify nobody." It may also be natural to Bloom's wise passivity. But Joyce is also articulating a larger vision of comic possibility in and through language, to be appraised in full once Bloom's revelations are spelled out.

A likely site for Bloomian cryptography occurs in "Calypso," in his response to signs inscribed on an envelope: "Two letters and a card lay on the hallfloor. He stooped and gathered them. Mrs Marion Bloom. His quickened heart slowed at once. Bold hand. Mrs Marion" (4.243–245). "Bold hand" characterizes the audacity (in 1904) of using a woman's given name, after "Mrs," in lieu of her husband's, but the phrase also cites the offender in sound-alike code. The "Bold hand" belongs to "Boylan," a linkage arrayed like a couplet rhyme in Bloom's subsequent exchange with Molly:

– Who was the letter from? he asked.
     Bold hand. Marion.
– O, Boylan, she said.   (4.310–312)

As elsewhere, Molly's exclamation opens its rounded window of revelation, here on the forbidden name, but Bloom continues to murmur the vocabulary of necessary avoidance. "His eyelids sank quietly often as he walked in happy warmth. Boland's breadvan delivering with trays our daily but she prefers yesterday's loaves turnovers crisp crowns hot" (4.81–83): "happy *warmth*," juxtaposed to "Boland's," stirs the verbal fire of *blazes* under the *Boylan* rhyme, touched again in the last word, "hot." Yet the boiling point of this verbal stew is never reached, there are no spillovers, for Bloom's usage seeks to relieve the pressure of awful facts by releasing them in code. Again, in "Lestrygonians": "He walked on past Bolton's Westmoreland house. Tea. Tea. Tea. I forgot to tap Tom Kernan" (8.371–372). Here the echo of "Boylan" in "Bolton" moves Bloom's thoughts through all the goods offered by William Bolton & Co.
– Grocers and Tea, Wine and Spirit Merchants – ahead to the hour for "Tea," the liaison at 4:00 p.m. That is the time

for the "tup," the animal copulation Bloom sees in Boylan's coupling with Molly, but he seems equally to summon and deflect that awful prospect here through the neutral rhyme on "tap."

Concealing rather than revealing, this echoing art seems to reverse the thrust of the Freudian slip, yet the change bears witness to Joyce's own studied apprehension of linguistic psychology. The really important things cannot be said, or cannot be said directly, and so must be left on the edges of verbal consciousness, like intimations that vanish when looked at directly. The secret wraiths are glimpsed as it were through the cracks of language, through the difference of respelled words. The principle of difference in Saussurian linguistics becomes the key to meaning here. In line with his adaptation of Freudian psychology, Joyce has shifted the mode of disclosure from theatrical spectacle to lexical subtlety, the medium of revelation from the stage to the page.

A proof of Joyce's motive and its intricate artistry lies not only in repetition and consistency but in the canny self-awareness his text displays about the practice. Consider Bloom's version of events during the last days of Parnell, whose followers stormed the offices of the anti-Parnellite paper, *United Ireland*, to set up their own *Insuppressible*: "[Bloom] saw [Parnell] once on the auspicious occasion when they broke up the type in the *Insuppressible* or was it *United Ireland*" (16.1333–1335). The historical record includes nothing about a breaking up of type in the newspaper office; that invention points suggestively toward the art of scrambled letters in Joyce's own text, his breaking down and respelling of crucial words, those broken tokens of revelation. They show the stress-fractures of *insuppressible* psychological pressure, a force Joyce invokes for this usage as he allows that incorrect but signal word to erupt, like the insuppressible secret in the Freudian slip, into Bloom's account of the incident. No less dramatically, no less cagily, he invokes the same values and methods in "Wandering Rocks," as "Mr Bloom turned over idly pages of *The Awful Disclosures of Maria Monk*, then of Aristotle's *Masterpiece*. Crooked botched print" (10.585–586): letters need to be tilted, canted, botched, in order to permit awful disclosures.

If the Freudian slip proceeds through speech, Joycean revelation also comes through typography, and the author gestures toward its potential for disclosure, appropriately, by manipulating letters and spaces on the printed page. In "Eumaeus," Bloom's copy of the evening paper is suggestively retitled: "The pink edition extra sporting of the *Telegraph* tell a graphic lie lay, as luck would have it ..." (16.1232–1233). Joyce's own *graphic* lies, not at all vivid, emerge entirely as a function of *writing* and printing, which allow the letters of the words for unspeakable fears to be recomposed, the spirit thus to be composed.

This art reveals its benefit in a passage immediately following that graphic signal, where Joyce likewise identifies print as the medium of attention. Bloom is scanning the ads in that copy of the *Evening Telegraph*: "First he got a bit of a start but it turned out to be only something about somebody named H. du Boyes, agent for typewriters or something like that" (16.1238–1240). Bloom's "start" registers the presence of Hugh Boylan, in "H. du Boyes," but it is a revelation *manqué*, a soft-focus insight, a look-alike that disappears into the difference between these words and his obsession. The mollifying effect is indeed the benefit of type, one which Bloom equally experiences and assigns to its dispensing medium here: the Boylan wraith, it turns out, is only an agent for typewriters – and type the agent of his relief.

Le non dit: that which is not said in *Ulysses* commands at least as much attention – and artistry – as what gets expressed. If this novel claims its landmark status in the history of the genre by taking those originally opposite forces of epic scheme and contemporary detail up to and through the resolution point, it pushes the revelatory powers of language into and past the expressible: it finds words, indeed, for what is not said. That this art serves interests and values more centrally and profoundly human than the conceit of these techniques is testified by a number of passages, where Joyce affirms the poetics and deepens the ethic of the "graphic lie."

In "Aeolus," for example, in the section headed "Orthographical," Joyce turns the sound of the printing machine into an unspeakable word and identifies print as the medium that fosters the rules of disclosure favored here − the necessary obliquity of words for urgent things:

> Sllt. The nethermost deck of the first machine jogged forward its flyboard with sllt the first batch of quirefolded papers. Sllt. Almost human the way it sllt to call attention. Doing its level best to speak. That door too sllt creaking, asking to be shut. Everything speaks in its own way. Sllt.   (7.174 177)

"Sllt" affords at once a type of the creaturely need to speak and, as printed, an example of Joyce's own art of scrambled letters, his expressive code of non-words. "Still it was a kind of language between us" (13.944), Bloom muses after his voyeuristic exchange with Gerty; "All a kind of attempt to talk" (11.1196), he muses on the motives and uses of music. The most moving things are mute − young Dignam thinks of his dying father's tongue moving silently behind his teeth (10.1171) − and so move to a non-normative language for disclosure.

These attitudes and practices induce a serio-comic view of the human condition. Linguistic spirits run high, but verbal products are tinged by the pathos of inexpressibility, and yet the very inadequacy of words spurs the energies of verbal invention. This mixed condition finds a suitably complex record in "Lestrygonians," as Bloom, fantasizing himself a waiter in a high-class hotel, engages in antic scramblings of his client's name:

> Wouldn't mind being a waiter in a swell hotel. Tips, evening dress, halfnaked ladies. May I tempt you to a little more filleted lemon sole, miss Dubedat? Yes, do bedad. And she did bedad. Huguenot name I expect that.   (8.887−890)

Here Joyce sends all the familiar signals of Bloom's look-alike word-play: "tip" calls up "tup," its sexual content charged by the prospect of "halfnaked ladies." Indeed, words seem to crackle with the energy of referents they can cite without naming. And so a name respelled to read "and she did bedad" seems already to utter Molly's "yes"; to affirm the positive, curative force in Bloom's nominal substitutions, the wish-fulfillments and compensations of coded words, which also serve here to appease his paternalistic need: yes, do be (a) dad. That such consolations are sheerly verbal, however, is the grimmer inference of Miss Dubedat's Continental background. Hers is a "Huguenot" or "hug-you-not" name. (This respelling is prompted more directly later, in "Sirens," when the word appears next to Aaron Figatner's, the inveterate misspelling of which is conscious knowledge for Bloom, whose "dark eye read Aaron Figatner's name. Why do I always think Figather? Gathering figs, I think. And Prosper Loré's huguenot name" [11.149–150]; here the "blessed virgins Bloom's dark eyes went by" certainly hug him not, as the cool blue-and-white consolations of the divine mother are recalled lovingly but achingly: "Bluerobed, white under, come to me" [151–152].") The hug-you-not name may be no replacement for the absence of love in Bloom's life, yet Joyce concedes the very uselessness of language in the word that shows its compensations most wonderfully. The energy of such artifice seems indeed to redeem, at least to alleviate, the conditions of its begetting.

That the rhythms of verbal invention work to the purposes of comic reconciliation is suggested in "Oxen of the Sun," in the cosmic vision of Joyce's Thomas de Quincey pastiche. Mixing Bloom's phrases into the high romantic diction, the narrative lifts young Milly into celestial array, surrounding her with a "mysterious writing" to signal the presence in this verbal prospect of Bloom's own magic language – the secret words of memory and desire, the coded tokens of fantasy and wish-fulfillment:

How serene does she now arise, a queen among the Pleiades, in the penultimate antelucan hour, shod in sandals of bright gold, coifed with a veil of what do you call it gossamer. It floats, it flows about her starborn flesh and loose it streams, emerald, sapphire, mauve and heliotrope, sustained on currents of the cold interstellar wind, winding, coiling, simply swirling, writhing in the skies a mysterious writing till, after a myriad metamorphoses of symbol, it blazes, Alpha, a ruby and triangled sign upon the forehead of Taurus.

(14.1102–1109)

An earthlier version of this "mysterious writing" has already signed Bloom into the strand, in "Nausicaa," as "A," that is, "Alpha." Writing himself into the skyscape here allows that capitalized verbal counter to stand provocatively and powerfully against a lower-case evocation of "blazes" Boylan (just as modernists punctuate rhetorically, all markings in cryptograms are significant). That their conflict might be danced to Bloomian triumph among the stars is perhaps the finest of those "myriad metamorphoses of [verbal] symbol" that occur in Bloom's words.

The ultimate benefice of this "mysterious writing" appears at the end of "Circe." Here Bloom conjures a prospect to fulfill his profoundest wish — a growing son, Rudy — by reciting the oath of secrecy in the Freemason's rite: "(*he murmurs*) ... swear that I will always hail, ever conceal, never reveal, any part or parts, art or arts" (15.4951–4952). The rubric of that secret society rhymes perfectly with Bloom's. rule of oblique disclosure. As he "*stands on guard, his fingers at his lips in the attitude of secret master*" (4955–4956), his signal for silence makes the summary gesture in the poetics of avoidance. This is the efficacious Word, the one that summons the secret image of his desire: the figure of Rudy now "*appears slowly, a fairy boy of eleven, ... holding a book in his hand*" (4956–4959). That the boy "*reads from right to left inaudibly*" (4959) identifies Hebrew as the language, his text most likely the Haggadah, the telling or revealing; reversing the conventional direction of (English) print, Joyce is suggesting the operation of code, more expansively, the coded nature of all revealings, Rudy preeminently. Here is the son recovered, not according to the logic or plot of the Homeric Nostos (though it adds wonderful resonance), but as the signal achievement of Joyce's searching experiments with human psychology and linguistics.

P(ost) S(criptum) U(lysses)

In a diary entry of 1941, Virginia Woolf reports an earlier conversation with T. S. Eliot, who has invoked the difficulty – indeed the impossibility – of writing in the wake of *Ulysses*. For Eliot the final episode of the book represents a *tour-de-force* that renders silence the only possible imaginative response. While these remarks may betray the anxiety of Joyce's influence on *The Waste Land*, which followed the model of *Ulysses* in shifting several characters-in-voice around a central underlying myth, the predicament the poet expresses here must be sensed with far greater gravity and acuteness by a novelist. Already in 1923, Eliot can look back at the history of the genre and, from the perspective afforded him by Joyce's inventions, announce that the novel has already ended with Flaubert and James. Mimetic reliability, verbal transparency, serial plot, linear development of themes usually congruent with the middle-class mores of its reading public, psychological insight into characters who change in ways that do not threaten their credibility, and the moral authority of a superior narrator: these are the features of the novel at its climacteric, in the classic age of realism in the second half of the nineteenth century, but they cannot survive the colossal novelty of *Ulysses*. How to extend work in a genre that no longer exists – at least as a productive basis for imitation and variation – is the challenge *Ulysses* poses to those writing after it. This dilemma is the finer point of "P.S.U.," the little cryptoglyph Ezra Pound used to designate the post-1922 era of the novel: efforts in the old genre appear to be only post-scripts to *Ulysses* – second thoughts, negligible remainders.

It is nonetheless impossible to discuss the fiction of the last seventy years without reference to the central, ramifying influence of Joyce's example. A list of minor works *un*affected by *Ulysses* might well be shorter than one naming the major novels obviously indebted to Joyce's opus. It is not the fact but the quality of influence that merits critical consideration – and discernment. Discrimination needs to be made in particular between works that merely imitate the surface mannerisms of *Ulysses* and those that master the challenge framed by Eliot and Pound; that extend the tradition of the new. For the imaginative possibilities Joyce opened in *Ulysses* are not necessarily advanced by the mere replication of techniques like "stream of consciousness" and "multiple perspective," the catch-phrases that conjure the standard examples of post-Joycean work in the usual narratives of literary history. These techniques are all too easily assimilated to work that affirms the social and aesthetic standards of the traditional novel, which – speaking in the language of ideal forms – asserts a middle-class morality and the attendant sense of individualism as a non-disruptive variation; that is, as a force held in *private*. The social totality to which Joyce's individuals are reconciled is of course a thing made, an imaginative construct, indeed as idiosyncratic as those radical subjects Bloom and Stephen. Its language – in the stylistic exercises of the second half of the novel – is humane but antic, as uncivil by any standard definition as Molly's monologue, which reads as its consummation. That Joyce ceased to call *Ulysses* a "novel" in mid-1918, moreover, just as the work was shifting its center of gravity from a narrative of character and incident to an exercise in styles, suggests that the forces driving his work past the standards (both social and artistic) of the traditional genre find their realization in the handling of language. Fiction that extends the Joycean project will participate in this energy.

The three writers cited here define a range of the ways in which major work negotiates the challenge of *Ulysses*. There is a para-Joycean, Virginia Woolf, who reproduces the techniques of *Ulysses* but develops a verbal consciousness in directions significantly different to Joyce's; there is the hyper-Joycean, Anthony Burgess, who exaggerates the mannerisms of Joyce and, in doing so, shows the real threat Joyce's linguistic art poses to the traditional novel and the social contract it often ratified; and there is the re-Joycean, Samuel Beckett, who revisits the linguistic conditions of *Ulysses* to conduct those rites of verbal comedy for which Joyce provides promise and prelude. A verbal carnival, conducted with the sort of somber gusto that Joyce's philosophy of language enjoins on a sympathetic spirit, will provide model and standard for the real Joycean legacy.

"I have read 200 pages [of *Ulysses*] so far," Virginia Woolf writes in her diary for 16 August 1922, and reports that she has been "amused, stimulated, charmed[,] interested ... to the end of the Cemetery scene." As "Hades" gives way to "Aeolus," however, and the novel of character and private sensibility yields to a farrago of styles, she is "puzzled, bored, irritated, & disillusioned" – by no grand master of language, in her characterization, but "by a queasy undergraduate scratching his pimples." No artifact of elite difficulty, *Ulysses* becomes for Woolf the "illiterate, underbred book ... of a self taught working man," a class-spectacle on which she summons the proper company: "*we all* know how distressing *they* are, how egotistic, insistent, raw, striking, & ultimately nauseating" (emphases added). Tellingly, Woolf's disaffection begins in the chapter that witnesses the erosion of the private individual's verbal sensibility, where Joyce has relocated the center of linguistic energy in the public realm of the newspaper. This fact lends a measure of rightness to the class identification she fixes on *Ulysses* – at least from the perspective of one disturbed by the force Joyce unleashes in that episode and amplifies through the rest of the book: the immanent anarchy (to Woolf) of a public (an underclass) given the power of speech, the custody of the tongue. Here indeed is the peril *Ulysses* poses to the social compact written into the history of the novel: the individuality privileged by the middle- or upper-middle-class situation of many early readers in the genre (reading, unlike speaking or listening, is solitary) suffers its demise from this point in *Ulysses*. This enterprise certainly threatens the social privilege into which Virginia Stephen was born; as a woman writer, whose models of *literary* authority are far fewer than Joyce's, she is, perhaps understandably, unwilling to forgo that privilege. In any case, she will not extend the work of *Ulysses* in ways that share in its essential energies. Her achievements are considerable, but they are not Joycean.

It is a testament equally to the influence of *Ulysses* and Woolf's own intellectual complexity that she tries to write a novel in the manner of the one she has just condemned. Virtually concurrently with those remarks of August 1922 she has begun to compose *Mrs Dalloway* (1925). Here her practices of multiple perspective and stream of consciousness, her compression of fictional events into a single day (in the middle of June), all show the immediate and local presence of *Ulysses*. But her novel is perhaps most interesting (in this critical context) in the way it fails to present an experience manifestly at odds with the social conventions and mental demeanor of its namesake, heroine, and controlling consciousness. Clarissa Dalloway, wife of a highly placed member of the government, never meets Septimus Warren Smith, veteran and psychic casualty of the Great War. Their joint presences in the novel are balanced and made possible by the technique of simultaneous narration or multiple perspective that *Ulysses* has recently exemplified for Woolf. Septimus's non-entry into Mrs. Dalloway's social sphere may be designed by Woolf as a symptom of the avoidances and vacuities of high society, but his distress exerts no great pressure on the language Woolf crafts as his monologue – a usage all too consonant with the balances and decorum of Mrs. Dalloway's, a high dialect not unlike the one into which the author was born. Whether this is a failure of imaginative nerve on Woolf's part, or her conscious refusal to enter the alternate dimension of his psyche, there is a restraint that sets the whole effort identifiably to the side of Joyce's main initiatives in *Ulysses*, a model otherwise so manifestly present in her novel.

The contours of the following passage merit scrutiny, especially where the voice of Septimus's incipient madness appears to enter Woolf's narrative. The modulation between his inward monologue and the narrative is exquisitely textured, but the difference between the two disappears into the tonic consciousness of Woolf the artist. She composes the passage

aesthetically and recomposes the character psychologically —
subduing the distress to a verbal music that finishes into a
healing closure, a settling repetition:

> Look the unseen bade him, the voice which now communicated
> with him who was the greatest of mankind, Septimus, lately taken
> from life to death, the Lord who had come to renew society, who lay
> like a coverlet, a snow blanket smitten only by the sun, for ever
> unwasted, suffering for ever, the scapegoat, the eternal sufferer, but
> he did not want it, he moaned, putting from him with a wave of his
> hand that eternal suffering, that eternal loneliness.

Joyce's verbal experiments are compelled by the psychology of
necessary avoidance, at least in Bloom's confrontation with
his private anxiety, but the author of *Ulysses* presents such
avoidance strategically, consciously, as an aspect of dramatic
character, not as the aim and function of narrative intervention.

The pressure of consensus in *Mrs Dalloway* is at once a social
theme that Woolf displays and a force she succumbs to. This
normative perspective gives the narrator some moral jurisdiction
over the plight of Septimus, but it also cancels the full presence
and ultimate validity of that experience in the novel. This
compromise finds its most telling sign in the narrative voice-
over during his last moment before suicide:

> There remained only the window, the large Bloomsbury-lodging house
> window, the tiresome, the troublesome, and rather melodramatic
> business of opening the window and throwing himself out. It was
> their idea of tragedy, not his or Rezia's (for she was with him).

Whether this action follows a high "idea of tragedy," or is
merely a "rather melodramatic business," the theatrical tropes
fit like generic characterizations around the otherwise poor,
bare, *un*accommodated animal of his psyche. Those phrases
do not emanate from Mrs. Dalloway's sensibility, for she sees
nothing of the scene, but from Woolf's narrator. They read
like a reflex action, a self-protective gesture on Woolf's part
(she would take her own life in 1941); they exercise the kind
of labeling and stabilizing force that may add to the pathos
of his uncontrol, but surely not to the reality of his death. Her
method here, holding the individual against the type, shares

in that sense of "proportion" − the lack of this, according to Septimus's psychiatrist, is his gravest danger − that is the essential social faculty, one that adjusts self to other and relates the individual to the larger social *res*.

To oppose the social contract of the old novel with the ferocity and terror of Anthony Burgess's *A Clockwork Orange* (1963) seems to go far beyond the gently recondite rebellions of *Ulysses*. Joyce's shifting of linguistic energy to the unruly mass of the common tongue nonetheless conforms to the same force that Burgess taps and amplifies in this futurist fantasy. Joycean scholar as well as novelist, Burgess clearly draws on the verbal and stylistic example of *Ulysses*, using language musically, impressionistically, almost as a sensory medium of its own. Most disturbingly, he turns the physical body of words toward social uses Joyce might hardly have intended − but still provided for, at least according to the severe critique by Wyndham Lewis (to whose report Joyce gave grudging credit).

In Lewis's analysis, the musication of language that Joyce indulges in *Ulysses* (and extends in *Finnegans Wake*, then "work in progress") participates in the main energies − or susceptibilities − of modern mass culture. Cartoonist and ideologue, Lewis portrays the ear as the intellectual soft spot in the body politic, the weak point through which Joyce seeks to manipulate his listener-reader. Whereas the eye separates the viewer from the object of sight and so affords the image and emblem of valid (aristocratic) individuality, the ear merges the auditor with the acoustic stimulus, and this process of sensory empathy provides channel and paradigm for bonding between persons in modern mass society. A body politic swayed to music, its members are dangerously suggestible, all too readily incited by sound to violent collective action. This is the sensory and social dynamic of common-man fellowship, Lewis avers, and to him it accounts for the demotic gigantism that plagues modern political history. No less a caricature than Lewis's analysis, Burgess's novel seems compelled to show the deep truth of Lewis's cartoon: exaggerating the powers Joyce has released, it provides a full, suitably complex testament to those energies in *Ulysses* that dismay middle-class moralities.

For Lewis the sounds of language are continuous with the worst effects of music, and so the organs and actions of speech afford him material for rich satire: talk is imaged as a sensuous flow into which the listener merges, losing the faculty of intellectual discrimination, conceptual definition. These perceptions reappear in the words Burgess coins for the parts of human speech − in the ideolect of his fictional state: "mouth" is *rot*; "sound" is *zwook*; "lips" are *goobers*; "voice" is *goloss*; "word" is *slovo*; to "listen" is *slooshy*, etc. Speech is a fluid integument issuing from the rotting mouth; words are slovenly inaccuracies that work only as material tokens, sensuous instruments for somatic provocation. In this acoustic sensorium bodies are melded into gangs, like the narrator-protagonist's, that prowl the futuristic waste land, their fellowship intoned and celebrated in his refrain "o my brothers." The sensual prodigality induced by sound is consummated through symphonic music, as in the dream the narrator experiences in listening eyelessly ("eyes" are *glazzies*, ever glazed) to Beethoven's Fifth:

Then brothers, it came. Oh bliss, bliss and heaven. I lay all nagoy to the ceiling, my gulliver on my rookers on the pillow, glazzies closed, rot open in bliss, slooshying the sluice of lovely sounds ... As I slooshied, my glazzies tight ... I knew such lovely pictures. There were vecks and ptitsas, both young and starry, lying on the ground screaming for mercy, and I was smecking all over my rot and grinding my boot in their litsos. And there were devotchkas ripped and creeching against walls and I plunging like shlaga into them, and indeed when the music, which was one movement only, rose to the top of its big highest tower, then, lying there on my bed with glazzies tight shut and rookers behind my gulliver, I broke and spattered and cried aaaaaaah with the bliss of it.

The conversion of language into music; the making of words into acoustic units with multiple or indeterminate significance: the whole Joycean linguistic project emerges in *Clockwork Orange* as a profoundly disturbing social force. Thus, as the narrator plays Joyce-wise with the opening words of the poem Beethoven used in the choral symphony, he exercises a license that spells out the true dangers of Joycean freedoms: "Joy, thou glorious spark of heaven, / Daughter of Elysium" becomes "Boy, thou uproarious shark of heaven, / Slaughter of Elysium."

While Burgess exaggerates the social consequences of Joyce's verbal art, as it were fanning the fire from the top, Beckett relives the linguistic predicament on which Joyce's artifice turns, sharing in its problematic at the primary level and reaching resolutions appropriately qualified, grimly genuine. In the monumental trilogy composed in the late 1940s and published through the early 1950s, *Molloy, Malone Dies,* and *The Unnamable,* Beckett pushes the language past what now appears as the merely stylized fluidity of Molly Bloom: here are words for the quicksilver moment of consciousness, the instant at which the human creature starts into speech and shows himself as both the glory and jest of creation. In prose that runs like a thin tracer-line along the unconscious, Beckett writes both dramatically and discursively, extending the discourse that Stephen initiates in "Proteus" and Bloom continues in "Nausicaa," enacting the principles that his meditation presents engagingly, joco-seriously.

Stephen's initial vision of an individual subject authoring and controlling stable relations between single words and integral referents is already dispatched by the title, *The Unnamable,* which proceeds to present the old thesis as the text for a little play, as a set of postulates performed for this nonce. "Make abundant use of the principle of parsimony," Beckett's speaker counsels himself for this uncharacteristic exercise in short simple sentences, where the limited size of the verbal unit coincides suggestively with the definition of self: "Assume notably henceforward that the thing said and the thing heard have a common source … Situate this source in me." That Beckett retails these hopes through imperatives, not even in the optative subjunctive, measures the force needed to put forward values no longer tenable. It is indeed the disintegration of the individual subject, as verbally constituted, that Beckett is recording and listening to.

Thus the Self, fabled as the source of verbal definition, appears (as that last passage continues) as no Adam naming the animals, rather as the kind of geriatric cretin now famed as Beckett's speaker-protagonist:

Carry if necessary this process of compression to the point of abandoning all other postulates than that of a deaf half-wit, hearing nothing of what he says and understanding even less. Evoke at painful junctures, when discouragement threatens to raise its head, the image of a vast cretinous mouth, red, blubber and slobbering, in solitary confinement, extruding undefatigably, with a noise of wet kisses and washing in a tub, the words that obstruct it.

To these difficulties may be added the problem of deferral, the postponement of meaning, the post-structuralist *différance* – "at no moment do I know what I am talking about ... The essential is never to arrive anywhere." This verbal not-as-yet locates the intellectual space Beckett owns: waiting. This interval is leased perpetually through speech, which can neither stop – "I'll go on [talking]" is the last phrase of the *Unnamable* – nor reach the referents it ever displaces. Here language operates as an apparently autonomous force, as the mechanism Joyce envisioned and set in motion through the stylistic exercises in the latter part of *Ulysses*. The engine whirs in the void the articulate individual once filled; the verbal ego Stephen Dedalus lost to the autonomous forces of language is lost to the *perpetuum mobile* of words, again and again, by Beckett's speaker, "who is I, who cannot be I, of whom I can't speak, of whom I must speak, that's all hypotheses, I said nothing, someone said nothing, it's not a question of hypotheses, it's a question of going on, it goes on ..." After such knowledge, what forgiveness?

"Whereas the leg condemned to the increase of pain inflicted by work knew the decrease of pain dispensed by work suspended, the space of an instant ...": Molloy's "space of an instant," this interval, this Beckettian place in time, defines a point between the two phases of the cycle, the twin mechanisms of energy and entropy, and it may point to a moment freed from the machine. Molloy continues: "I hobble, listen, fall, rise, listen and hobble on, wondering sometimes, need I say, if I shall ever again see the hated light ..." The force and effect of that little appositive is immense, for he need not say *need I say*: between the headlong energy of language and the declining fortunes of the corporeal machine, it enters gratuitously, a grace note, perhaps the only effort to be made at redemption. At the center of Beckett's universe, I am suggesting, as at one center of *Ulysses*, stand the rival claims of gratuity and necessity. It is an issue Beckett decides on the side of the angels. "The words are everywhere, inside me, outside me, well well": to the encompassing machine of language the last fillip throws itself, a futility full of grace. If it is a provisional gesture, its value is secured by the dominance of that which it opposes. Well well. How like an Irish writer of the English language.

Appendix: Joyce's schema for Ulysses

Title	Scene	Hour	Organ	Art	Colour	Symbol	Technic	Correspondences
I Telemachia								
1 "Telemachus"	The Tower	8 a.m.		Theology	White, gold	Heir	Narrative (Young)	*Stephen*: Telemachus, Hamlet *Buck Mulligan*: Antinous *Milkwoman*: Mentor
2 "Nestor"	The School	10 a.m.		History	Brown	Horse	Catechism (Personal)	*Deasy*: Nestor *Sargent*: Pisistratus *Mrs O'Shea*: Helen
3 "Proteus"	The Strand	11 a.m.		Philology	Green	Tide	Monologue (Male)	*Proteus*: Primal Matter *Kevin Egan*: Menelaus *Cocklepicker*: Megapenthus

II Odyssey

	Scene	Time	Organ	Art/Science	Colour	Symbol	Technique	Correspondences
4 "Calypso"	The House	8 a.m.	Kidney	Economics	Orange	Nymph	Narrative (Mature)	*Calypso:* The Nymph *Dlugacz:* The Recall *Zion:* Ithaca
5 "Lotus-eaters"	The Bath	10 a.m.	Genitals	Botany, Chemistry		Eucharist	Narcissism	*Lotus-eaters:* The Cabhorses, Communicants, Soldiers, Eunuchs, Bather, Watchers of Cricket
6 "Hades"	The Graveyard	11 a.m.	Heart	Religion	White, black	Caretaker	Incubism	*Dodder, Grand, & Royal Canals, Liffey:* The Four Rivers *Cunningham:* Sisyphus *Father Coffey:* Cerberus *Caretaker:* Hades *Daniel O'Connell:* Hercules *Dignam:* Elpenor *Parnell:* Agamemnon *Menton:* Ajax
7 "Aeolus"	The Newspaper	12 noon	Lungs	Rhetoric	Red	Editor	Enthymemic	*Crawford:* Aeolus *Incest:* Journalism *Floating Island:* Press
8 "Lestrygonians"	The Lunch	1 p.m.	Esophagus	Architecture		Constables	Peristaltic	*Antiphates:* Hunger *The Decoy:* Food

	Scene	Hour	Organ	Art	Colour	Symbol	Technic	Correspondences
9 "Scylla and Charybdis"	The Library	2 p.m.	Brain	Literature		Stratford, London	Dialectic	*The Rocks*: Aristotle, Dogma, Stratford *The Whirlpool*: Plato, Mysticism, London *Ulysses*: Socrates, Jesus, Shakespeare
10 "Wandering Rocks"	The Streets	3 p.m.	Blood	Mechanics		Citizens	Labyrinth	*Bosphorus*: Liffey *European Bank*: Viceroy *Asiatic Bank*: Conmee *Symplegades*: Groups of Citizens
11 "Sirens"	The Concert Room	4 p.m.	Ear	Music		Barmaids	Fuga per Canonem	*Sirens*: Barmaids *Isle*: Bar
12 "Cyclops"	The Tavern	5 p.m.	Muscle	Politics		Fenian	Gigantism	*Noman*: I *Stake*: Cigar *Challenge*: Apotheosis
13 "Nausicaa"	The Rocks	8 p.m.	Eye, Nose	Painting	Grey, blue	Virgin	Tumescence, detumescence	*Phaeacia*: Star of the Sea *Gerty*: Nausicaa
14 "Oxen of the Sun"	The Hospital	10 p.m.	Womb	Medicine	White	Mothers	Embryonic development	*Hospital*: Trinacria *Nurses*: Lampetie, Phaethusa *Horne*: Helios *Oxen*: Fertility *Crime*: Fraud

15 "Circe"	The Brothel	12 midnight	Locomotor apparatus	Magic	Whore	Hallucination	*Circe*: Bella

III *Nostos*

16 "Eumaeus"	The Shelter	1 a.m.	Nerves	Navigation	Sailors	Narrative (Old)	*Skin the Goat*: Eumaeus *Sailor*: Ulysses Pseudangelos *Corley*: Melanthius
17 "Ithaca"	The House	2 a.m.	Skeleton	Science	Comets	Catechism (Impersonal)	*Eurymachus*: Boylan *Suitors*: Scruples *Bow*: Reason
18 "Penelope"	The Bed		Flesh		Earth	Monologue (Female)	*Penelope*: Earth *Web*: Movement

Further reading
Text, background, interpretation

Text

The first legal editions of *Ulysses* did not appear in English-speaking countries until 1934, in the United States, and 1936, in the United Kingdom. These editions were marked with problems stemming from the circumstances surrounding the first edition, published by Shakespeare and Company, Paris, 1922; Joyce's last-minute revisions and additions had set great difficulties for the French printer, Maurice Darantiere. Subsequent impressions of this edition included lists of errata, but these seemed hardly complete, and not all mistakes would be set right in subsequent editions, which introduced variants of their own. A history of these editions is provided in *ULYSSES: A Critical and Synoptic Edition*, 3 volumes, Hans Walter Gabler *et al.*, eds. (New York and London: Garland, 1984), 1855–1856. This list is augmented, and most of its descriptions challenged, by John Kidd, in "An Inquiry into *Ulysses: The Corrected Text*," *Papers of the Bibliographic Society of America*, 82 (December 1988), 509–514. Of these editions (ten by Gabler's count, seventeen by Kidd's) the most widely distributed were the English (Harmondsworth: Penguin, 1968) and the American (New York: Random House, 1961). The trade edition of Gabler's text (New York: Vintage, 1986; London: Bodley Head, 1986, 1993) is the most frequently used at present.

Gabler departs from usual Anglo-American editorial practice insofar as he forgoes the use of a conventional "copy-text," a printed edition that serves as basis for variation and emendation. In its place Gabler constructs a "compound" or "continuous" manuscript out of the many fair-copies, corrections, and additions in Joyce's hand. Given the difficulties surrounding the first editions of *Ulysses*, this principle appears reasonable, and it seems to suit Joyce's emergent concept of authorship particularly well: *Ulysses* appears as a "work in progress," the phrase Joyce used for *Finnegans Wake* during most of the seventeen years he was writing it. Of course the reading text generated by this "continuous" manuscript is riskier than one relying on the authority of a conventional copy-text; Gabler's principles seem to suggest that editing is no less a process than the composition of the text, and editorial revisions might well take their place in such a process. Nonetheless, Kidd has launched virulent attacks on Gabler's version and the method on which it is based, and has invoked the absolute rationale of the copy-text (presumably the editorial method for his own forthcoming edition of *Ulysses*, its appearance frequently promised and postponed over the last several years). The value of Kidd's contribution will be assessed whenever his edition appears.

Background

Works of historical scholarship useful for Joyce studies include Conor Cruise O'Brien, *Parnell and His Party, 1880–1890* (Oxford: Clarendon, 1957); Malcolm Brown, *The Politics of Irish Literature: From Thomas Davies to W. B. Yeats* (Seattle: University of Washington Press, 1972); George Dangerfield, *The Damnable Question: A Study in Anglo-Irish Relations* (Boston: Little, Brown, 1976); F. S. L. Lyons, *Culture and Anarchy in Ireland, 1890–1939* (Oxford: Clarendon, 1979); Paul Bew, *Conflict and Conciliation in Ireland, 1890–1910* (Oxford: Clarendon, 1987); R. F. Foster, *Modern Ireland, 1600–1972* (London: Allen Lane, 1988), esp. 400–515; Foster, "Anglo-Irish Literature, Gaelic Nationalism and Irish Politics," in *Ireland after the Union* (Oxford: Oxford University Press, 1989; published for the British Academy), 61–82.

Relevant works in the history and theory of the novel include George Lukács, *The Theory of the Novel: A Historico-philosophical Essay on the Forms of Great Epic Literature* (1920), trans. Anna Bostock (1971; rpt. Cambridge, Mass.: MIT Press, 1977); Mikhail Bakhtin, *The Dialogic Imagination: Four Essays* (1934–35), ed. Michael Holquist, trans. Caryl Emerson and Michael Holquist (Austin: University of Texas Press, 1981); Ian Watt, *The Rise of the Novel: Studies in Defoe, Richardson, and Fielding* (Berkeley: University of California Press, 1957); Joseph Frank, *The Widening Gyre: Crisis and Mastery in Modern Literature* (New Brunswick: Rutgers University Press, 1963), esp. 3–62; John Halperin, ed., *The Theory of the Novel: New Essays* (New York: Oxford University Press, 1974), esp. Halperin, "The Theory of the Novel: A Critical Introduction," 3–22, and A. Walton Litz, "The Genre of *Ulysses*," 109–120; David Sidorsky, "Modernism and the Emancipation of Literature from Morality: Teleology and Vocation in Joyce, Ford, and Proust," *NLH*, 15 (Autumn 1983), 137–153; Nancy Armstrong, *Desire and Domestic Fiction: A Political History of the Novel* (New York: Oxford University Press, 1987); Brian G. Caraher, "A Question of Genre: Generic Experimentation, Self-Composition, and the Problem of Egoism in *Ulysses*," *ELH*, 54 (Spring 1987), 183–214; Robert Martin Adams, *Afterjoyce: Studies in Fiction After Ulysses* (New York: Oxford University Press, 1977).

Some of the contemporary works relevant to Joyce are available in more recent editions: Samuel Butler, *The Authoress of THE*

ODYSSEY (1897), ed. and intro. David Grene (Chicago: University of Chicago Press, 1967); Charles Lamb, *The Adventures of Ulysses* (1808), ed. John Cooke (1892; rpt. Edinburgh: Split Pea Press, 1992), with Afterword by Alistair McCleery and Ian Gunn; *James Connolly: Selected Writings*, ed. P. Berresford Ellis (New York: Monthly Review Press, 1973).

The standard biography is by Richard Ellmann, *James Joyce* (1959; rev. New York: Oxford University Press, 1982). The most concise guide to local and topical allusions in *Ulysses* is by Don Gifford, with Robert J. Seidman, *ULYSSES Annotated: Revised and Expanded Edition* (Berkeley: University of California Press, 1988).

Interpretation

Ulysses has received more critical attention than any modernist text. This commentary is as various as the centers of attention in Joyce's book, but the interpretive emphases have tended to develop in a now recognizable pattern. The initial difficulties in understanding the book led critics to emphasize the importance of Joyce's schema; this tradition culminated in a number of works published in the early 1970s (coinciding with the half-century anniversary of *Ulysses*). A counter-current emerged in the 1970s with post-structuralist criticism, which turned attention to Joyce's play with language and style. These concerns continue to generate commentary, but the newest initiatives seek to return *Ulysses* to primary contexts in local and world history, thus to describe its sociological and ideological content. These three areas of concern define issues for discussion, not fixed positions; emphasis on the importance of the schema in the early phase, for example, is countered in the same years by critics who assert the values of realism, the force of documentary reportage in *Ulysses* (a difference beginning in the early 1920s with rival appreciations by Eliot and Pound). None of these phases is airtight, each defines a vital area of awareness in *Ulysses* and so a topic of constant relevance (my analysis attempts to synthesize all three), but the three-fold scheme may be used to organize a list of secondary readings.

Major works extending and complicating and opposing schematic criticism, in the first phase, include Ezra Pound, "Paris Letter: *Ulysses*," *Dial*, 6 (June 1922), 623–639; T.S. Eliot, "*Ulysses*, Order and Myth," *Dial*, 7 (November 1923), 480–483; Stuart Gilbert, *James Joyce's ULYSSES: A Study* (1930; rpt. New York: Vintage, 1952); F.R. Leavis, *The Great Tradition* (1948; rpt. New York: Doubleday, 1954), 39–40; Hugh Kenner, *Dublin's Joyce* (1956; rpt. Boston: Beacon, 1962); A. Walton Litz, *The Art of James Joyce: Method and Design in ULYSSES and FINNEGANS WAKE* (New York: Oxford University Press, 1961, 1964); Robert Martin Adams,

Surface and Symbol: The Consistency of James Joyce's ULYSSES
(New York: Oxford University Press, 1962, 1967); Stanley Sultan,
The Argument of ULYSSES (Columbus: Ohio State University Press,
1964); David Hayman, *ULYSSES: The Mechanics of Meaning* (1970;
rev. Madison: University of Wisconsin Press, 1982); Richard Ellmann,
Ulysses on the Liffey (New York: Oxford University Press, 1972,
1973); Clive Hart and David Hayman, eds., *James Joyce's ULYSSES:
Critical Essays* (Berkeley: University of California Press, 1974); Michael
Seidel, *Epic Geography: James Joyce's ULYSSES* (Princeton:
Princeton University Press, 1976).

Attention to language and style in the second phase features major
work by Marilyn French, *The Book as World: James Joyce's ULYSSES*
(Cambridge, Mass.: Harvard University Press, 1976); Hugh Kenner,
Joyce's Voices (Berkeley: University of California Press, 1978);
Kenner, *ULYSSES* (London: Allen and Unwin, 1980); Karen
Lawrence, *The Odyssey of Style in ULYSSES* (Princeton: Princeton
University Press, 1981); Fritz Senn, *Joyce's Dislocutions: Essays on
Reading as Translation*, ed. John Paul Riquelmé (Baltimore: Johns
Hopkins University Press, 1984); Derek Attridge and Daniel Ferrer,
eds., *Post-structuralist Joyce: Essays from the French* (Cambridge:
Cambridge University Press, 1984); Jean-Michel Rabaté, *James
Joyce, Authorized Reader* (1984; rev. and trans. Baltimore: Johns
Hopkins University Press, 1991). Some of these books show the direct
influence of French post-structuralism, a development aptly surveyed
in relation to Joyce studies by Geert Lernout, *The French Joyce* (Ann
Arbor: University of Michigan Press, 1990).

Work focused on the historical and social contexts of *Ulysses* and
its ideological content, in the third phase, includes Colin MacCabe,
James Joyce and the Revolution of the Word (London: Macmillan,
1979); Dominic Manganiello, *Joyce's Politics* (London: Routledge
and Kegan Paul, 1980); Bonnie Kime Scott, *Joyce and Feminism*
(Bloomington: Indiana University Press, 1984); Cheryl Herr, *Joyce's
Anatomy of Culture* (Urbana: University of Illinois Press, 1986);
Vicki Mahaffey, *Reauthorizing Joyce* (Cambridge: Cambridge
University Press, 1988); Robert Spoo, *Joyce and the Language of
History: Dedalus's Nightmare* (New York: Oxford University Press,
1994).

Two different but equally important works on Joyce's process of
composition are by Frank Budgen, *James Joyce and the Making of
ULYSSES* (1934; rpt. Bloomington: Indiana University Press, 1960),
and Michael Groden, *ULYSSES in Progress* (Princeton: Princeton
University Press, 1977). A good introductory reading comes from
C. H. Peake, *James Joyce: The Citizen and the Artist* (London:
Arnold, 1977). A useful gathering of essays addressing the standard
range of critical topics in Joyce studies has been made by Derek

Attridge, ed., *The Cambridge Companion to James Joyce* (Cambridge: Cambridge University Press, 1990).
  Articles mentioned here are grouped according to topic:

(1) *The Odyssey:*
W. B. Stanford, "The Mysticism That Pleased Him: A Note on the Primary Source [Lamb's *Adventures of Ulysses*] of Joyce's *Ulysses*," *Envoy: A Review of Literature and Art*, 5 (April 1951), 62–69; Hugh Kenner, "Homer's [Butler's] Sticks and Stones," *James Joyce Quarterly*, 6 (Summer 1969), 285–298; Joseph A. Kestner, "Before *Ulysses*: Victorian Iconography of the Odysseus Myth," *JJQ*, 28 (Spring 1991), 565–615.

(2) Modernism:
A. Walton Litz, "Pound and Eliot on *Ulysses*: The Critical Tradition," *JJQ*, 10 (Fall 1972), 5–18; Christopher Butler, "Joyce, Modernism, and Post-modernism," in Attridge, ed., *The Cambridge Companion to Joyce* (q.v.), 259–282; Hugh Kenner, "Modernism and What Happened to It," *Essays in Criticism*, 37 (April 1987), 97–109; Robert Scholes, "Joyce and Modernist Ideology," in Morris Beja and Shari Benstock, eds., *Coping with Joyce: Essays from the Copenhagen Symposium* (Columbus: Ohio State University Press, 1989), 91–107.

(3) History, politics, and popular culture:
Robert Tracy, "Leopold Bloom Fourfold: A Hungarian–Hebraic–Hellenic–Hibernian Hero," *Massachusetts Review*, 6 (Spring–Summer 1965), 523–538; Carol Schloss, "Choice Newseryreels: James Joyce and the *Irish Times*," *JJQ*, 15 (Summer 1978), 325–338; Fredric Jameson, "*Ulysses* in History," in W. J. McCormack and Alistair Stead, eds., *James Joyce and Modern Literature* (London: Routledge, 1982), 126–141; Jeremy Hawthorn, "*Ulysses*, Modernism, and Marxist Criticism," in McCormack and Stead, eds., *James Joyce and Modern Literature* (q.v.), 112–125; Joseph Buttigieg, "The Struggle against Meta(Phantasma)-physics: Nietzsche, Joyce, and the 'Excess of History,'" in Daniel O'Hara, ed., *Why Nietzsche Now?* (Bloomington: Indiana University Press, 1985), 187–207; Robert Spoo, "'Nestor' and the Nightmare: The Presence of the Great War in *Ulysses*," *Twentieth Century Literature*, 32 (Summer 1986), 137–154; G. J. Watson, "The Politics of *Ulysses*," in Robert D. Newman and Weldon Thornton, eds., *Joyce's ULYSSES: The Larger Perspective* (Newark: University of Delaware Press, 1987), 39–58; Garry M. Leonard, "Women on the Market: Commodity Culture, 'Femininity,' and 'Those Lovely Seaside Girls,'" in Thomas F. Staley, ed., *Joyce Studies Annual* (Austin: University of Texas Press, 1991), 27–68.

(4) Speech and writing:
Derek Attridge, "Joyce's Lipspeech: Syntax and the Subject in 'Sirens,'" in Morris Beja *et al.*, eds., *James Joyce: The Centennial Symposium* (Urbana: University of Illinois Press, 1986), 59–65; Jacques Derrida, "*Ulysses* Gramophone: Hear say yes in Joyce," in Bernard Benstock, ed., *James Joyce: The Augmented Ninth* (Syracuse: Syracuse University Press, 1988), 27–75; Patrick A. McCarthy, "Joyce's Silent Readers," in Bonnie Kime Scott, ed., *New Alliances in Joyce Studies* (Newark: University of Delaware Press, 1988), 73–78; Joseph Valente, "The Politics of Joyce's Polyphony," in Scott, ed., *New Alliances* (q.v.), 56–69.

(5) Gender issues:
Derek Attridge, "Molly's Flow: The Writing of 'Penelope' and the Question of Women's Language," *Modern Fiction Studies*, 35 (Autumn 1989), 543–565; Suzette Henke, "Joyce's New Womanly Man: Sexual Signatures of Androgynous Transformation in *Ulysses*," in Janet E. Dunleavy *et al.*, eds., *Joycean Occasions: Essays from the Milwaukee James Joyce Conference* (Newark: University of Delaware Press, 1991), 46–58.